LITERARY STRUCTURES
Edited by John Gardner

WEDGES

AND

WINGS

The Patterning of
Paradise Regained

By Burton Jasper Weber

Foreword by John Gardner

SOUTHERN ILLINOIS UNIVERSITY PRESS
Carbondale and Edwardsville

Feffer & Simons, Inc.
London and Amsterdam

Library of Congress Cataloging in Publication Data

Weber, Burton Jasper.
  Wedges and wings.

  (Literary structures)
  Includes bibliographical references and index.
  1. Milton, John, 1608–1674. Paradise regained.
I. Title.
PR3565.W3   821'.4   74–20703
ISBN 0–8093–0673–5

Copyright © 1975 by Southern Illinois University Press
All rights reserved
Printed in the United States of America
Designed by Gary Gore

For Peggy

Contents

Foreword

Wedges and Wings is a book I'm extremely proud to have helped toward publication. Like other books in the Literary Structures series, it is intended not for specialists — though specialists will find it illuminating — but for teachers, students, and "the general reader," by which I mean anyone who enjoys great poetry and would like to enjoy it more fully. Granted, the general reader of poems like *Paradise Regained* may no longer exist. If so, the reason must have something to do with the pressure of college courses, the only place such a poem as this is likely to be introduced; or it has to do with changes in literary taste, or changes in the attitudes of civilized people toward traditional Christianity. Whatever the reasons for the poem's decline in popularity, the fact is that *Paradise Regained* is still one of the greatest poems in English, a poem no teacher, student, or general reader can resist if he's properly introduced to it. That proper introduction — or so it seems to me — is what this book provides.

Professor Weber makes plain — and therefore moving — what goes on in *Paradise Regained*. To say that his reading of the poem is original would be to suggest that Milton has failed to communicate with generations of readers, which I doubt. But it is true, I think, that Professor Weber has laid out the structure of the poem in a way most of us have only intuited, that he has sorted through the critical opinions, testing, weighing, balancing, synthesizing, adding insights of his own, and has come up with a rich and elegant reading that ought to send the most hardened skeptic back to Milton's text, back to old notions of beauty and nobility in poetry.

As in his earlier book for this series, *The Construction of Paradise Lost,* Professor Weber works chiefly with the logic of the poem—how it's built, how part works against part, and so on—and makes a convincing, satisfying case simply because, to put it bluntly, he has the clearest mind now at work in the field of Milton studies. But *Wedges and Wings* has a further virtue: it's not only useful and correct but a pleasure to read.

Specialists will find that this book does not reflect all the latest opinions of Milton scholars—which, personally, I think to be a blessing, on the whole. The book has been a long time in the works. Partly this is because I, the editor, have been away from my desk, traveling and writing novels, and partly it is because Professor Weber, while he was writing this book, was in the process of going blind. After his blindness became total, I myself read through the recent Milton criticism and, finding nothing not implicitly answered already in the work he had done, urged him to publish what he had on hand without further ado. As a Milton scholar he has advantages beyond his meticulous rationality and good sense, by the way: he has for some time been writing what I at least consider first-rate poetry of his own. He is presently busy with, besides poetry, a collection of essays on Shakespeare.

JOHN GARDNER

Boskydell Road, Carbondale, Illinois
May 1974

Preface

I think I had better explain at the start what I have tried to do in this study, since, for one thing, my method is not entirely orthodox — or at least its orthodoxy is not entirely visible — and for another thing, what interests me in Milton seems to be a little unfashionable.

When I set out to examine the structure of *Paradise Regained* I made no assumptions about whether the form had to be a narrative, a meditation, or, say, a *débat*. Instead I tried to determine the nature of the poem's organization. To put it all a little stiffly, I asked myself, "Is the focus on the characters, and do their natures account for the number, kind, and order of their speeches? Is the focus on the ideas themselves, and does the logic of the argument account for the number and nature of the speeches?" When I had considered this preliminary question, I tried to determine what concepts were implied by the arrangement of the materials: "Can temperance account for the divisions of these arguments? Magnanimity? The Platonic tripartite soul?" Formulating a hypothesis, I looked especially at the structure of the separate speeches, the argumentative motifs common to a series of offers, and the replies of Jesus insofar as these could suggest the significance of Satan's temptations. (Since Jesus would fall if he did not answer accurately, his answers must be true assessments of the attacks.) While examining the text, I consulted critics and scholars, and gratefully borrowed whatever helped to explain details of argument or character.

What I have recorded is not my procedures but my results — a theory about the patterning of *Paradise Regained*. I hope that in explaining this theory I do not sound arbitrary, for each detail of my reading has been preceded by a weighing of alternatives, some proposed by others, some invented by myself. Each detail has been reconsidered many times. Elizabeth Pope describes thus the exegetical tradition concerning Christ's temptation in the wilderness: "There is nothing about the tradition more remarkable than the way its authorities keep within a limited circle of clearly defined themes or ideas. They are like children who have been given a certain number of blocks to play with: they select, and discard, and arrange in different patterns; but they always use the same blocks." Examining *Paradise Regained* has been like that: a perpetual selecting, discarding, and shuffling of colored blocks.

In this undertaking I have proceeded like any empiricist—like an astronomer, say. Not assuming that planets must travel in circles, he tries epicycles and ellipses, and in the process develops a hypothesis; he checks his data, he consults the data of other astronomers, and finally he records what he hopes is a consistent, comprehensive, and elegant theory on planetary motion. Neither my procedure nor this analogy is likely to win me any friends nowadays. In these romantic times it is generally accepted that ambiguity—the ability of a work to suggest multiple meanings—is a more valuable quality than orderliness; consequently the critic who examines the coherence of a work is thought simple- and narrow-minded: praise goes to the man who seeks and affirms a richness of diverse—even incompatible—alternatives. Yet it is a strange and not altogether admirable scientist who accepts the astronomical theory of the angel Raphael: that the incomprehensibility of the heavens is the mark of their grandeur, that contrary astronomical theories are equally probable and equally unprovable, that the stars are arranged in a deliberately misleading way. I do not see why literary critics should be any less concerned to discriminate and test critical hypotheses than astronomers to prove and disprove theories of planetary motion.

If my labor has been like an astronomer's, I hope that my results resemble a formal analysis by a critic of music. As the critic himself knows, formal analysis does not provide a total account of a piece: it may distinguish between a perfunctory and an extended development section, but it does not distinguish a dull from a moving theme. In relation to a complex and profound movement, however, a formal analysis can provide an alternative to the perception of random and disconnected details—of a dissonance here, a syncopation there. It can help the listener to understand the pattern by which the details are ordered, and increase the number of details he can comprehend.

I know, then, that structural criticism has its limitations. It may overemphasize the structural intricacy of a work dull in style or thought, it may neglect those elements which do not bear directly on the structure of a moving work, but which create its power. Nevertheless, formal analysis is helpful to the reader of a work like *Paradise Regained,* a work which is not only complicated but which in its sublimity is inaccessible and abstruse. The atomizing pedant in Pope (Alexander, not Elizabeth) subverts what is for Pope the end of criticism: to show "How part relates to part" and "they to whole,/ The body's harmony, the beaming soul." I have tried to give that kind of holistic account of the structure and meaning of *Paradise Regained.*

A version of the first chapter of this book appeared as an article, under the title "The Schematic Structure of *Paradise Regained:* A Hypothesis," in the *Philological Quarterly,* Vol. 50, No. 4 (October 1971). I would like to thank the University of Iowa for permission to reprint it, with revisions. In order to make the book more accessible to the nonspecialist, I have used a modernized text of *Paradise Regained,* that edited by Douglas Bush and contained in *The Complete Poetical Works of John Milton* (Boston, 1965). I wish to thank the publishers, Houghton Mifflin Company, for permission to quote from this edition.

I would like to express my gratitude to Janice Moulton, William Main, and Carl Dennis—two colleagues and a visitor from abroad; their aid, encouragement, and friendship helped me through the bleak period coincident with the writing of this book. I am deeply indebted to John Gardner, not only for his meticulous criticism of my manuscripts and for his helpful advice, but for his long-term faith and interest in my work.

BURTON J. WEBER

Regina, Saskatchewan
February 1974

1

Wedges

AS ARNOLD STEIN has observed,[1] *Paradise Regained* begins with an audacious joke: "I who erewhile the happy garden sung,/ By one man's disobedience lost, now sing/ Recovered Paradise to all mankind" (1. 1–3). By his witty allusion to Vergil's "I am the man who once played a melody on the shepherd's slender pipe," [2] Milton asserts the sublimity of *Paradise Regained: Paradise Lost* is a mere pastoral by comparison. He returns to the point in each of the poem's formal images.

Three sets of these compare *Paradise Regained* with other examples of epic. The three extended similes which describe Satan's desperation before the offer of Rome (4. 10–24) form one such set. The third simile, which likens Satan to waves shattering against a rock, alludes to the description of the embattled Mezentius in the *Aeneid*. The second, the comparison of Satan to a "swarm of flies" around a winepress, recalls the *Iliad*'s description of the warriors fighting for Sarpedon's body. Given the allusive context, a phrase in the first of the images — "a man who had been matchless held/ In cunning" — evokes the opening of the *Odyssey*. In a second figurative passage, Milton compares the Parthian troops displayed by Satan to the armies besieging Albracca in Boiardo's epic (3. 337–44). Finally, when imagistically describing the attendants of Satan's banquet (2. 350–61), Milton couples general references to classical demigods and nymphs with specific references to the "fairy damsels" met by Malory's heroes, Lancelot, Pelleas, and Percivale ("Pellenore"). Equating the two sorts of figures — the first

1

are "feigned of old," the second "fabled since"—Milton suggests a likeness in genre: classical fables prefigure the chivalric romance. Each set of allusions designates a subclass of epic, for though Milton specifically mentions incidents in the *Orlando Innamorato*, he calls up Spenser with the archaisms "prowest" and "paynim," and names a form rather than a specific poem: "as romances tell." Comparing *Paradise Regained* to the modern epic, the romance (medieval and decadent classical), and the classical epic (Roman and Greek), Milton sets the poem against the entire history of the genre.[3]

His epic, he implies, is superior: its armies are bigger, its spirits fairer. By the trivial surface comparisons Milton invites a serious consideration of the ways in which *Paradise Regained* differs from its rivals. The Renaissance epic contains the erotic interest exemplified in the pursuit of "The fairest of her sex, Angelica," but in *Paradise Regained* there is no such material (Belial raises the subject and is promptly snubbed). The classical epic contains world travels and wars for kingdoms, but in *Paradise Regained* their place is taken by an exploration of ideas and a war of words. The romance contains religion embellished by pagan mythology or by medieval superstition, but *Paradise Regained* presents true and unadorned religion. The poem is sublime because, meeting Plato's objections to poetry, Milton eschews "popular" sources of appeal, "please[s]" and "affect[s] the rational principle in the soul," and does not center on "the passionate and fitful temper, which is easily imitated." [4] Even *Paradise Lost* is not so pure: that poem presents the passion of Adam for "the fairest of her sex," it includes a classical battle, it contains mythological adornments in the persons of Sin and Death.[5]

There are two schools of thought about the structure of *Paradise Regained.* The first, the schematic school, finds the poem's order-giving principle in the arrangement of conceptual materials. E. M. W. Tillyard, for example, claims that *Paradise Regained* is "not an epic"—for, he argues, it lacks events and "liv[ing]" characters; asserting that its long speeches are "void of dramatic interest," he compares the poem to a morality play.[6] Louis Martz views the poem as a meditation, a nondramatic didactic work.[7] The second school, the dramatic school, locates the order-giving principle in the relationship and development of the characters. Stein, the most impressive exponent of this view, attacks as "over-systemat[ic]" an attempt at schematic explanation,[8] and accounts for the order of temptations on the basis of psychology.[9]

Both schools are faulty in their rejections—the poem contains both dramatic and nondramatic elements—but surely Tillyard is right in feeling that the argumentative materials predominate. It is easier to find logical justifications for the number and kind of temptations in the second day's trial than to find psychological explanations so strong as to necessitate each step in that long debate. The subordination of drama follows from Milton's pursuit of sublimity: a poem in which passion and activity are eschewed and argument and doctrine emphasized is bound to stress sentiments more than character and plot.

In an examination of the schematic patterning of *Paradise Regained,* the first question to be answered is where the logical divisions of the poem occur. The second day's trial has been variously divided. Elizabeth Pope argues that the banquet scene and offer of glory stand apart from the temptations of the world,[10] and Irene Samuel suggests a general resemblance of the day's offers to the four kinds of imperfect kingdom described by Plato in *The Republic.*[11] More systematically, Barbara Lewalski has grouped the offers in a 3–3–1 pattern,[12] Northrop Frye in a 2–2–3 pattern,[13] Howard Schultz in a 1–4–2 pattern,[14] and A. S. P. Woodhouse in a 1–5–1 pattern.[15] Not only has this complex day been variously analysed, but even the placement of the poem's central divisions has been questioned. Mrs. Lewalski has revived earlier disputes by arguing that the banquet scene which opens the second day's trial contains the references to the Israelites and the prophets which typify the first day's trial,[16] and Dick Taylor, Jr., has opened a similar dispute about the storm scene which opens the third day's trial, arguing that it continues the second temptation.[17]

The central divisions of the poem, though, *are* clearly marked. The fact that the banquet scene is separated from the first day's trial by a set of introductions is evidence, as Gilbert long ago observed,[18] that the first section of *Paradise Regained* ends at the end of the first day. The end of the second day's trial provides a natural dividing point, and the evidence of a continuous action ending just before the pinnacle episode is not strong enough to obliterate this division. Taylor argues that after the offer of learning, Satan forms a new plan to induce Jesus to accept the kingdoms of the world through the use of omens, that he thereupon makes an astrological prediction (4. 374–93), creates a storm (4. 394–450) to provide evidence, and completes his plan by interpreting the storm as proof of his prediction (4. 451–83).[19] But as Taylor acknowledges,[20] this unified action requires that several conflicting pieces of evidence be disregarded, first the statement before Satan's astrological prediction that Satan is "at a loss" (4. 366) and the statement before Satan's interpretation of the storm that he has "no new device" (4. 443), and second the authorial assertion that the storm is designed to "tempt the Son of God with terrors dire" (4. 431). If these lines are taken seriously, the episodes must be differently interpreted. If Satan is "at a loss" when he makes his prediction, that prediction is no stratagem but a feeble assertion of knowledge and power in retraction of what Satan has just revealed about his mental exhaustion and impotence (he has tried everything he can think of, he admits: "wealth . . . honor, arts . . . arms,/ Kingdom . . . empire . . . life contemplative [and] active . . . glory . . . fame" [4. 368–71]; and he has gotten nowhere: "I found thee [in the wilderness] . . . And thither will return thee" [4. 372–74]). The speech thus marks the end of Satan's attempt to use rational persuasion to induce Jesus to accept the world, and it demonstrates the failure of Satan's own reason. The storm, if it is meant to "tempt . . . with terrors," has no connection with the prediction, but is a new approach. When it fails, Satan tries to coerce Jesus with an ominous interpretation of the incident. The attempt is a makeshift one, as is shown by its reuse of the face-saving prediction (4. 467–80), and for this reason it may be said to be the product of an exhausted mind, a mind with "no new device"; the speech is not, then, the conclusion of a thought-out plan. When the episodes are read in the way the authorial commentary suggests, the connected action proposed by Taylor vanishes, and with it the reason for dividing the poem at a point later than the end of the second day's trial.

The secondary divisions of the poem are suggested by the relation of the biblical events to Milton's account. The biblical episodes occur in the beginning of the first day's trial, at the end of the third day's trial, and in the middle of the second day's trial; extrabiblical events end the first day's trial, begin the third day's, and both open and close the second day's trial. The placement of these materials suggests that Milton is expanding each day's trial into a triple trial mirroring the three days' series: *Abc aBc abC.*

In the first day, Satan's confession that he is indeed Satan (1. 357–405) must have—the patterning suggests—some relation to the second day's temptation, and his last speech, the request to return (1. 468–92), must relate to the third day's trial. In the third day, the storm scene must be related to the first day's trial, and Satan's ominous interpretation of it to the second day's trial. In the second day, the banquet scene and the offer of learning are the two main analogues to the other days' temptations, and because of the complexity of the second temptation, Milton provides particularly strong indications of the division. The banquet and the offer of learning stand apart because they alone are untraditional offers,[21] and parallel losses of temper by Satan are used to divide these two episodes from the rest; after the rejection of the banquet, Satan petulantly orders it removed (2. 392–403) and before the offer of learning he "impudent[ly]" tells Jesus the price for his kingdoms (4. 134–69). Loss of temper is suggested by the fact that both these maneuvers are self-defeating: the boastful order and the removal of the banquet by demons expose Satan's evil intentions nearly as blatantly as that later demand to which Jesus replies, "[P]lain thou now appear'st/ That Evil One, Satan for ever damned" (4. 193–94). These two incidents are the only ones of their kind (the speeches which follow the offer of Israel [3. 203–50] and the offer of learning [4. 365–94] are not fits of temper); they punctuate the action by interrupting the alternating arguments and counterarguments.

The poem's structural cues thus support Woodhouse's 1–5–1 division of the second day's trial. The five subsections of the center section, however, require some further grouping. One division which suggests itself is the separation of the three particular kingdoms from the two offers — wealth and glory — which are only indirectly connected with rule. Yet wealth and glory are not related to one another in the way that three kingdoms are, for one is a means and the other an end, as Jesus observes: "Thou neither dost persuade me to seek wealth/ For empire's sake, nor empire to affect/ For glory's sake" (3. 45–46). When the lack of parallelism is taken into account, a tripartite division suggests itself (means, end, and rule proper), the third member being itself divided in three (rule of Israel, Parthia, and Rome). The structural cues, in other words, point to a continually tripartite grouping of the second day's temptations:

$$
\begin{array}{lll}
a & & \\
b & 1 & \\
& 2 & \\
& 3 & \text{I} \\
& & \text{II} \\
& & \text{III} \\
c & &
\end{array}
$$

The second structural question is the significance of the structural units. Many different bases have been suggested for the division: Martz has divided the poem on the basis of rhetorical units, Mrs. Lewalski on the basis of the offices of Christ, Professors Schultz and Pope on the basis of types of temptation, and Woodhouse on the basis of kinds of sin.

In connection with his theory that *Paradise Regained* is not a dramatic poem but a didactic biblical meditation, Martz argues that the three temptations correspond to expository units: the first temptation is an introduction, setting out the terms of the meditation, the second temptation is the meditation,[22] and the third temptation is a peroration containing "prophecy, epiphany, and praise." [23] This division seems rather arbitrary. If Milton were using the first day's trial as exposition, Satan's second council would be an interim report: Satan has laid down the terms of the debate and is now prepared to develop his arguments. Instead, Satan is represented as having completed an unsuccessful trial and as preparing for a new assault (2. 140–46). If the storm and tower scene were part of an epilogue, Milton would not treat them as trials having the same function as earlier assaults: he says that the storm is a device to "tempt" Jesus, and through Satan's introduction he links the last attack with Satan's previous attempts to "understand" his "adversary" (4. 527). Furthermore, it is doubtful that the storm, the revelation on the tower, and the angelic hymn are to be grouped as "three symbolic scenes" which foretell the passion, last judgment, and millennium, as Martz suggests.[24] The angelic banquet is treated as a conclusion to the entire action, not as the last of three symbolic episodes (Mrs. Lewalski compares the scene to the "heroic victor's fit reward" which ends the Book of Job [25]), and the last lines of the poem connect the hymn and banquet with an event not explicable in terms of the millennium, the return of Jesus "unobserved/ Home to his mother's house" (4. 636–39).

Mrs. Lewalski much more plausibly identifies the three temptations with the Son's three offices, prophet, priest, and king.[26] There are, though, problems of evidence with her view. The overlapping of materials suggests that these offices are not a satisfactory basis of division; Mrs. Lewalski uses references to prophets in the dialogue to identify Jesus' office,[27] but such references are found not only in the first temptation but in the second, which should be devoted to the kingly office—not only in the banquet scene but, as Mrs. Lewalski observes, in the offer of learning.[28] Furthermore, the only evidence Mrs. Lewalski has for the identification of the third day's trial with the priestly office is a dubious symbolic reading of the last temptation. She argues that Satan's astrological prediction prepares for the identification of the storm scene with the prodigies at the death of Christ,[29] but she cannot adequately account for evidence which insists upon a literal reading of the incident—the fact that in reply to Satan's assertion that the "tempest" of the night "fore-signif[ies] and threaten[s] ill" (4. 460–66), Jesus asserts that these "signs" are "false portents" (4. 489–91). If the prodigies are to be taken as foreshadowing the crucifixion, then Jesus must be taken as erring in his rebuttal. In her identification of the tower scene with the crucifixion, Mrs. Lewalski cites Hall's connection of the violence of Christ's transportation with the violence of the crucifixion,[30] Andrewes's connection of Christ's ascent of the tower with the ascent of the cross,[31] Knox's connection of Satan's "Cast thyself down" with the cry of the Jews that Christ come down from the cross.[32] But Mrs. Lewalski cannot successfully demonstrate that these connections are made in *Paradise Regained.* The description of Satan transporting Jesus "without wing/ Of hippogrif" (4. 541–42) does not associate the ride with the torments of the crucifixion; the picture of the temple, a "mount/ Of alabaster, topped with golden spires" (4. 547–48), does not evoke the cross; and the connection of Satan's cry with the cry of the Jews relies on the usual interpretation of the tower episode—the interpretation which Milton rejected. The usual interpretation, as Mrs. Lewalski notes,[33] is that Christ was placed upon a safe perch and was tempted to make a miraculous descent. His position, thus, was like his position later when he refused to descend miraculously from the cross. If, as in Milton's account, Jesus is placed on a pointed pinnacle from which descent would seem inevitable, the likeness to the crucifixion situation is lost. (The likeness is particularly absent from the scene as Mrs. Lewalski interprets it, for, in arguing that Jesus does perform a miracle,[34] she imagines his doing what he refused to do on the cross.)

But the main objection to Mrs. Lewalski's theory concerns its thematic implications rather than its evidence. Because the offices apply only to God the Son, the organizational basis implies that *Paradise Regained* is either an historical or an ecclesiastical poem. When Miss Pope says that Milton "presents his work as a narrative of the facts," [35] she is voicing the historical view; such a view underlies explanations which make Jesus' conduct peculiar to his particular situation, explanations like Miss Samuel's argument that Jesus is too old to start a "course in world literature" and that he needs to judge the arts by their usefulness to him in his coming work,[36] or Gilbert's argument that Jesus is taught directly by God and therefore does not need what is "necessary to a mortal man who must do his work in a human fashion." [37] Schultz is the primary exponent of the ecclesiastical view, arguing that Milton gives "plain instruction to read his work as, before all else, a parable for the church." [38] Mrs. Lewalski adopts this view intermittently—when, for example, she interprets the offer of Rome as an attack on Catholic worldliness.[39]

It could be argued that these two kinds of interpretation misrepresent *Paradise Regained*. The historical interpretation defends the work by appeal to its weakest aspect; Jesus' denunciation of the mob (3. 49–56), for instance, has struck many critics as un-Christ-like—in fact Martz uses such passages to argue that Milton is writing a meditative rather than a representational poem.[40] Furthermore, as Miss Samuel suggests, the elaborateness of Jesus' replies cannot be accounted for simpy as attempts at historical realism: the method suggests an ethical aim.[41] As to ecclesiastical allegory, it is hard to see how the equation of Parthia with militant Protestantism [42] can account for the inclusion of such materials as Satan's elaborate description of the Parthian realm, or Milton's elaborate description of Parthian warfare (3. 269–97, 310–36); surely these do not allegorize the spread of Protestantism on the Continent and the manners of Protestant pamphleteers.

Schultz's reference to Donne's Third Satire [43] only calls attention to the difference between allegorical description and Milton's mode. In support of his reading, Schultz claims that literal interpretation of *Paradise Regained* entails such great absurdities that allegory is a necessity. He argues, for example, that the banquet scene cannot be taken literally because a banquet could not be expected to tempt a man who can resist the attraction of women; because when Satan looks backward upon his temptations (4. 368 ff., 536 ff.), he does not mention an offer of food; and because Jesus does not present a moral argument against gluttony in the way that he argues against money, power, and glory.[44]

But the fact that Jesus is shown to be hungry yet not starving (2. 252–56) introduces a test of gluttony, as Miss Pope observes,[45] and gluttony is referred to when Jesus says that he has no "need" for food (2. 318) and when he calls Satan's provisions excessive and showy, "pompous delicacies" (2. 390); Satan does refer to literal hunger in ending the banquet scene (2. 406–9), and though he does not mention food again, Jesus himself does, alluding, as Mrs. Lewalski says,[46] to the banquet scene in his description of a Roman feast (4. 113–20); and food is, of course, more tempting than sex to a man who is hungry. Schultz is no more persuasive in his other arguments against a literal approach to *Paradise Regained,* and in the absence of such proof, the claim that *Paradise Regained* is an allegorical poem is not very compelling.

The main objection to these two approaches is not that they are inapplicable, however, but that they impoverish the poem. As B. Rajan says, "what matters in a literary 'explanation' is not so much its consistency with the facts—there are other explanations which fit the facts as well and for some readers fit them more readily—as the standard of poetical achievement it implies." [47] A reader who accepts Gilbert's interpretation of the offer of learning can derive no moral significance from the argumentation: in this reading, the arguments prove only that superhuman beings have no difficulty in overcoming human trials. A reader who accepts Schultz's interpretation of the offer of learning can derive only a very specific and narrow sort of moral, that ministers need not be university graduates. [48] The loss entailed in such readings can be seen if these conclusions are juxtaposed to the issues which the offer raises for ethical critics like Stein, such general issues as the relation of learning to wisdom. [49]

The third basis for division, type of temptation, is used in different ways by professors Pope and Schultz. The former says that the first day's trial is a test by necessity, the second a test by pleasure, and the third a test by force. [50] The latter argues that the first day's trial is a trial by fraud, the second a trial by snares, the third a trial by terrors. [51] Both these versions have problems of evidence. In support of his basis of division, Schultz cites the angels' assertion that Jesus will face "whate'er may tempt . . . seduce,/ Allure, or terrify, or undermine" (1. 178–79), and Satan's opening assertion that he will use "Not force, but well-couched fraud, well-woven snares" to prevent Jesus' reign (1. 97). [52] The first of these lines, however, clearly does not function as an index, and the second does not provide the tripartite division Schultz supposes, since it is only an emphatic contrast of the two means usually associated with Satan, force and fraud, "fraud" and "snares" being synonyms used in emphatic repetition. And though it is true that the three days' temptations do differ in method, and though force is, as both critics suggest, the distinguishing mark of the third day's temptation, neither "fraud" nor "necessity" will serve to distinguish the first day's trials.

In the narrow sense in which Satan's shepherd's guise is fraud, fraud is also an aspect of the second day's temptation, in that Satan there disguises himself as a man "in city or court or palace bred" (2. 300), a man of the world paternally advising a lad from the country, as Stein puts it. [53] In the extended sense in which Satan in acknowledging his identity is "disguised" as an "angel of light"—so Schultz argues [54]— —Satan in the third temptation poses as an innocent bystander who had nothing to do with the storm of the preceding night (4. 450–54).

Disguise and falsehood are not confined to the first temptation. "Necessity," on the other hand, is too narrow to cover the events of the day, since it cannot account for the dialogue which follows Satan's opening ploy.

If the division of the poem by the Son's offices entails an underestimation of the meaning of *Paradise Regained,* the main difficulty with the division by kind of temptation is that it underestimates the poem structurally. Deceit, seduction, and duress, a classification based upon the circumstances surrounding the sin, is not so basic a division of sins as the traditional lust of the flesh, lust of the eye, and pride of life, a classification based upon the kind of sin. (The tradition involved is that of the triple equation, the tradition—treated extensively by Miss Pope —that "the three sins which Christ refused to commit were, in essence, the same three which had caused Adam's fall." [55]

It is improbable that Milton would abandon a profound basis of division to put a trivial one in its place; and the division proposed by Miss Pope is not only trivial but schematically weak: necessity, pleasure, and force do not sound like a systematic and inclusive classification. Miss Pope is ungenerous, surely, when she deduces Milton's reasons for ordering the poem in this way. She argues that Milton sacrificed the triple equation and adopted the untraditional order of temptations from Luke in order to obtain a dramatically effective close; then, in order to save the triple equation, he inserted a trial of flesh and a test of pride into the second day's trial, leaving, she says, a central division based upon type of temptation.[56] Yet, in her earlier discussion of the triple equation, Miss Pope notes that exegetes had to strain to apply lust of the flesh, lust of the eye, and pride of life in their proper order to the events in Matthew, and that these sins actually fit the bread-kingdoms-tower sequence in Luke better than they do the traditional bread-tower-kingdoms sequence of Matthew.[57] Instead of arguing that Milton chose a makeshift order for what are trivial ends, why should Miss Pope not deduce that Milton decided to preserve a morally significant and morally climactic classification by abandoning the traditional but intellectually unsatisfying order of events?

Kind of sin is the last basis upon which critics have divided *Paradise Regained.* This is the sort of basis provided by the triple equation, but unfortunately most critics have agreed with Woodhouse [58] that Milton rejected the patristic formulation, adopting the Protestant view that the first temptation is a temptation to distrust rather than a temptation to gluttony. Many follow Gilbert [59] in citing Calvin's argument that for a man to break a forty day fast with bread is not gluttony; several have argued, like Mrs. Lewalski,[60] that Milton eliminates hunger from the first temptation (see 2. 245–51) in order to make the issue a test of faith. Yet Milton places in God's mouth what seems to be the patristic formula: the Father announces that Jesus will overcome "Satanic strength/ And all the world, and mass of sinful flesh" (1. 161–62).

The statement sounds like an index, especially because the alteration of the usual wording ("the devil") serves to introduce what Miss Pope notes is Milton's unorthodox emphasis on violence in the tower scene,[61] and because during the third temptation, Satan's undisguised appearance makes his "strength" specifically "Satanic" (Satan is wryly described as flying "without wing/ Of hippogrif," that is, on his own wings, and the litotes indicates that the "wonted shape" in which he appears [4. 449] is, as Mrs. Lewalski says, [62] a fallen angel's shape, not, as Miss Pope suggests,[63] the human form used on the preceding days). Moreover, the elimination of hunger may be viewed in exactly the opposite way from the way that Mrs. Lewalski views it: as Milton's way of answering Calvin's objection and preserving the first temptation as a trial of the flesh. For if eating bread is not gluttony in a man hungry from forty days' fasting, it is gluttony in a man who has been miraculously preserved from hunger. This interpretation accords with Milton's handling of the same problem later in the poem. Miss Pope, who interprets the banquet scene as a test of gluttony, notes that Milton would have to meet Calvin's objections at this point.[64] What Milton does is to increase the elaborateness of the food as he increases the hunger of Jesus, thereby preserving the element of excess.

One advantage of the patristic formulation is that it allows a morally climactic arrangement. As Woodhouse's analysis shows, the Protestant formula would require opening with what is the most serious, and therefore the climactic, sin. Another advantage is that the patristic formula makes an inclusive classification of sins by reference to the faculties of the soul. This correlation is lost in Woodhouse's formulation, in which sins of the flesh are omitted, and pride of life doubly represented—as distrust in the first temptation and presumption in the third.[65] Other arrangements are possible—Mrs. Lewalski reads the banquet-money-glory series as containing an allusion to flesh, eye, and pride [66]—but none would preserve this classification as a basic division in the poem.

Though Stein says that Milton's Jesus has a "full, Platonic tripartite soul," [67] the division which Milton uses here is not, apparently, that which Miss Samuel says is typical of him, the Platonic division of desire, will, and reason.[68] In Plato, ambition is the aim of will, and will is the soul's middle faculty.[69] In *Paradise Regained* the love of glory is associated with the highest faculty; it is said to be particularly characteristic of God (3. 109–20), and it is associated with Satan's fall (3. 145–48), a connection, Miss Pope remarks, usually reserved for the tower scene when that scene is identified with the pride of life.[70] The division of the soul in which will is the highest rather than the middle faculty is the neo-Platonic sense-reason-intellect division expounded by Bembo in the fourth book of *The Courtier:* "from sense springs appetite, which we have in common with the brutes; from reason springs choice, which is peculiar to man; from the intellect, by which man is able to commune with the angels, springs will." [71]

Milton correlates these faculties with the temptations in differentiating Satan's three approaches. Emotive appeals are used in the trial of the flesh. What is distinctive about Satan's initial approach is his wheedling—" 'Tis true, I am that Spirit unfortunate" (1. 358), "From thee I can and must submiss endure/ Check or reproof, and glad to scape so quit" (1. 476–77); Stein has noted that in the first temptation, Satan tries "the plausible voice of fallen humanity," feigning humility and earnestness,[72] and that he tries "to soften up [his] opponent" with sincerity.[73] The offer of the world is a test of reason, and Satan here uses argumentation; even the lowest of the second day's temptations contains abstract arguments rather than emotive appeals: "These are not fruits forbidden; no interdict/ Defends the touching of these viands pure" (2. 369–70).

Taylor has noted that there is a tacit rule which governs Jesus' replies, that he may not merely refuse but must offer sound reasoning; [74] the rule follows from the nature of this particular trial. In the third temptation, Satan pits his will against Jesus' intellect, the use of force which typifies this temptation being the direct expression of perverted will.

The basic distinctions of the triple equation may be used to explain the five subsections in the center of the second day's trial, the subsections which are the heart of the offer of the world. Structural cues suggest that this section divides first into a tripartite group consisting of the offer of wealth, the offer of glory, and the offer of specific kingdoms. This group sounds as though it relates to the three faculties as these are associated with the three main temptations. Wealth goes with what is the lowest faculty in both the Platonic and the neo-Platonic systems; Plato describes the appetitive soul as "loving gain or money." [75] Glory goes with the intellect; and the kingdoms, which are most directly representative of the world, go with the reason, the faculty tried particularly in the second temptation.

The three kingdoms themselves form a tripartite group, and this
group too seems to bear some connection with the faculties: Israel as
God's chosen nation goes with intellect, Parthia as the savage kingdom
goes with the sense ("which we have in common with the brutes"), and
Rome as mistress of the world is most representative of worldly kingdom, and therefore appropriately connected with the reason. The
exact mode of relationship needs defining, of course, just as the relationship of each trial to the other days' trials needs defining; but the
overall pattern of the second day is nevertheless suggested:

$$
\begin{array}{lll}
A & & \\
B & a & \\
  & c & \\
  & b & c \\
  &   & a \\
  &   & b \\
C & &
\end{array}
$$

After the major units of the poem have been established, one final
question can be asked, whether the schematic structure does not extend further than the grouping of Satan's separate tests. The possibility has been broached by Taylor, who says that "No single incident"
in *Paradise Regained* "is concerned with only one kind of temptation,"
that each works on "multiple levels." [76] The particular motifs which
he mentions seem too miscellaneous to be worth pursuing: "obedience, trust, containment of identity, true liberty and true power in
opposition to false liberty and false power, the refraining from using
one's strength capriciously, and others";[77] but Miss Pope has noted
a quality of the banquet scene which is in fact suggestive.

In explaining what she says is confusing about the banquet, she
notes that the issue of godhood is fought out at length, that the description of the banquet suggests kingly luxury, and that the issue of
Jesus' hunger is raised; [78] the three elements she mentions relate to
the triple equation. If Taylor's generalization is correct, and if what
Miss Pope notes about a single episode applies to other episodes of
Paradise Regained, then the same structural principle by which Milton
incorporates the other two days' temptations within each day's trial
is present also within each episode: each of Satan's tests mirrors the
three days' series. The possibility must be taken seriously, for it is hard
to imagine why Milton would give to a minor offer, the banquet, a
complexity absent in the more serious trials. The reason for such an

intricate procedure, as well as for the analogous subdivision of the separate days' trials, lies in the tradition of significant temptation which Stein mentions as an important element in the drama of *Paradise Regained*.[79] In order to dramatize the fact that, as Stein puts it, "a single wrong move means ruin," [80] Milton turns each day's temptation, and each subsection of each day's temptation, into a test of the full neo-Platonic tripartite soul.

2

The First Try

MERRITT HUGHES argues that a Christianized version of Aristotelian magnanimity is the moral key to *Paradise Regained*,[1] but the poem's neo-Platonic structuring makes this hypothesis unlikely. The patristic formula used in the three temptations suggests the three theological virtues: faith, hope, and charity are opposites of devil, world, and flesh. But although the third temptation can plausibly be labeled a test of faith, and though the first trial can be construed as an appeal for misplaced charity—the suggestion is Northrop Frye's [2] —nevertheless the three virtues are inapplicable to several important passages in the poem. Jesus' praise of self-control (2. 466–72) does not relate to charity, and his praise of selfless worldly rule (2. 457–65) does not relate to hope.

Arnold Stein proposes as moral basis the Platonic cardinal virtues as they are treated in *The Republic*;[3] these too seem inapplicable. In *The Republic* courage is identified with the soul's middle faculty, the will,[4] and both the weight given courage as a typifying virtue and its middle placement are wrong for *Paradise Regained*, where, as Stein says, courage has "an entirely minor role" at the end of the poem.[5] The passage in the *Gorgias* which he mentions [6] *is* suggestive, though: "And will not the temperate man do what is proper, both in relation to gods and to men;—for he would not be temperate if he did not? . . . In his relation to other men he will do what is just; and in his relation to the gods he will do what is holy. . . . And must he not be courageous? for the duty of a temperate man is not to follow or avoid what he ought not, but what he ought, whether things or men or pleasures or pains, and patiently to endure when he ought." [7] Temperance here is the traditional "guardian of the threshold," [8] not that epitomizing virtue which Stein uses as his moral key; [9] it, justice, and holiness fit the neo-Platonic faculties, and not only is their sequence in the passage congruent with the poem's, but the citation of courage by way of afterthought corresponds to Milton's placement and subordination of that virtue (he treats it as an illustration of holiness, by antithesis to the violence which typifies Satan's perverted will).

The passages of the poem which offer the plainest definitions of these three central virtues occur in Jesus' rejection of the offer of wealth, his speech on the cessation of oracles, and his rejection of the offer of glory. In the first, Jesus defines temperance as control over the emotions, the "rul[ing]" of "Passions, desires, and fears" (2. 466–67). He opposes it to self-indulgence — "Subject[ion]" to "lawless passions" in the self (2. 471–72) — and to the overvaluing of sensory goods; for when he contrasts the man who "reigns within himself" with a literal "king" (2. 466–67), he is answering Satan's taunt about his low-born poverty (2. 415) with a rejection of royal luxury. In the second passage, Jesus by calling himself God's "Oracle" (1. 460–61) introduces the poem's identification of just rule with instruction — a democratic conception of rule which serves to connect the virtue of justice with the rightful functioning of the reason. Jesus opposes just rule to self-interested rule and to the pursuit of power over others, the first in his rebuke to Satan for using what true knowledge he has from God to increase his reputation with men (2. 444–54), the second in his rebuke to Satan for guiding men to their ruin (4. 434–44). The third passage defines holiness as conformity to God's will (3. 106–7) and opposes this virtue to vanity — self-interested idealism — and to misbelief. Vanity is rebuked in Jesus' contrast of actions done for God's glory with actions done for the glory of the doer, which go "unpraised" (3. 100–107); misbelief is attacked in Jesus' contrast of worldly fame with divine approval (3. 47–70).

Temperance is the subject of the first day's trial. That the sensory soul is being tested is suggested by the emotiveness of Satan's approach, as consistent here as his coerciveness in the third day's trial. The lack of rational persuasiveness in the arguments of the opening trial calls attention to this emotiveness. Satan's tribute to Jesus' note-worthiness and holiness is at variance with his request for material aid and for a distrustful miracle (1. 326–45), and the illogicality is pointed up by Jesus' replies. When Jesus says, "Why dost thou then suggest to me distrust,/ Knowing who I am" (1. 355–56), he is not acknowledging his identity, as A. S. P. Woodhouse suggests,[10] but disproving Satan's argument by internal evidence; for the fact that Jesus gives only indirect replies to the questions about his regal and divine status is what provides Satan with the opportunity for his subsequent probes. In his second speech, there is a transparent sophistry in Satan's claim that because he has no just motive for enmity to man ("[men] to me/ Never did wrong or violence" [1. 386–89]), therefore he is not their foe—transparent because the refutation lies in the converse of his words: he is their foe, since he did wrong and violence to them. In his third speech there is a similar sophistry: the claim that "not will/ But misery" caused Satan "to part from truth" (1. 468–74) contains the truth in converse: Satan's willful departure from truth caused his misery (Jesus has said that Satan was "composed of lies/ From the beginning" [1. 407–8]).

It is improbable that the blatant lies are intentional, part of an attempt to be "provocative"—the idea is Stein's [11]—for such an aim would be incompatible with Satan's appeals for trust and pity; the point seems, rather, that Satan is neglecting rational for emotional persuasion. In the last case, the turn from reproach ("Sharply thou hast insisted on rebuke" [1. 468]) to a less convincing obsequiousness ("But thou art placed above me" [1. 475]) shows that Satan is using his real resentment—he is inwardly "ang[ry]" and "disdain[ful]" (1. 466)—to make his opening specious plea sound plausible. Similarly, in the second case the fallacious proof is covered by the expression of a real pleasure in worldly power: "[I] dwell/ Copartner in these regions of the world,/ If not disposer" (1. 391–92). Howard Schultz, who interprets the opening trial as a temptation to distrust, says that Satan's initial disguise is that of the symbolic good shepherd,[12] but Milton does not stress the piety in Satan's opening pose, for, as Elizabeth Pope points out, he chooses not to give him the conventional guise of a pious hermit.[13] The pose he does attribute to Satan is appropriate for a test of temperance; the old shepherd is a man whose interests are appetitive—he is interested not in God or government but in food and warmth (1. 214–20)—and yet whose appetitiveness seems understandable and blameless—he seeks only a minimal existence (1. 338–41), and he lacks higher aims through circumstance rather than through degeneracy, being "curious . . . to hear" whatever "happens new" (1. 333–34). The illogicality in Satan's opening requests is concealed by the limitations of the man he is pretending to be, a man in whose mouth the requests sound, as Miss Pope says, "completely natural and even appealing." [14]

Jesus' control of his passions is contrasted with Satan's emotional appeals. Satan's appeals for sympathy in his second speech are juxtaposed to Jesus' "stern[ness]" (1. 406), and Satan's inner "anger and disdain" (1. 466) and the verbose dishonesty of his third speech are juxtaposed to Jesus' unemotiveness (he replies with "unaltered brow" [1. 493]) and to his terseness (it is pointed up by Milton's commentary on his three-line reply: "He added not" [1. 497]). As the emotiveness in Satan's temptations serves to label the trial as a test of the sensory soul, the imperturbability of Jesus recalls the virtue which relates to that faculty, temperance.

But Satan in the first trial tests whether "the temperate man" will "do what is proper, both in relation to gods and to men"; the first assault is directed primarily at the sense, but, given the opportunity by Jesus' indirect replies, Satan subsequently tests the temperate man's justice and holiness, therein anticipating the trials of the second and third days. The first set of speeches is frequently misread. Many critics argue, like Miss Pope,[15] that Jesus' first reply is a rejection of distrust summarized in its last two lines: "Why dost thou then suggest to me distrust,/ Knowing who I am, as I know who thou art?" (1. 355–56). These last lines, however, are not a summary. Jesus' speech consists of three separate points, that God's word is more important than the bread Satan asks (1. 347–51), that Jesus can fast as Moses and Elijah did (1. 351–54), and that distrust is inappropriate for the Son of God (1. 355–56); "then" in the final lines means not "consequently," introducing a summary, but "furthermore," introducing the last point in a series. Moreover, the final lines are not the main argument in the speech. The third point is paired with the first: both are interrogative ("Think'st thou such force in bread? Is it not written?" runs the first),[16] and both contain attacks on Satan's disguise (the first is, "For I discern thee other than thou seem'st"); the middle point, nonparallel, is set apart. The first and third points are indirect retorts; the second point is direct and final. Thus the third point is subordinated, and the second argument emphasized. That argument concerns appetite rather than distrust. Many critics feel that Satan's opening request is not appetitive, but the fact that only the first of the day's temptations directly mentions food places emphasis on the sensory appeal.

The second set of speeches concerns government primarily. The climax of Jesus' speech is, of course, his pronouncement about the cessation of oracles (1. 454–64), and it replies to what is the central argument in Satan's speech: the opening concession, Satan's acknowledgment of his identity (1. 358–86), only prepares for his next argument, that he is not men's foe (1. 387–96); and his closing confutation, his denial of the charge of envy (1. 397–405), is only a supporting argument for the assertion of friendliness. The point of the claim of friendship is, as Stein says, that Satan "has a business relationship with man" and "so may have something to offer"; [17] the hint anticipates Satan's second day's offers of worldly power, and Jesus' identification of himself as God's "living Oracle" anticipates the explanation of rule which he gives in rejecting the offer of wealth:

> [T]o guide nations in the way of truth
> By saving doctrine . . .
> Is . . . more kingly [than external rule]; this attracts the soul,
> Governs the inner man, the nobler part,
> That other o'er the body only reigns,
> And oft by force, which to a generous mind
> So reigning can be no sincere delight.
>
> (2. 473–80)

The final set of speeches, which primarily concern religion, prefigure the third day's trial. Satan's request to return (1. 478–92) is the central part of the speech—it is the new proposal, while the other portions of the speech look backward—and it includes an invitation for Jesus to act like God: "Thy Father . . . suffers the hypocrite . . . To tread his sacred courts . . . ; disdain not such access to me." Jesus' brief reply emphasizes the religious issue, for he expands his answer to the invitation—"I bid not" (1. 495)—with a religious explanation: "do as thou find'st/ Permission from above; thou canst not more" (1. 495–96). The last speeches are analogous to the climactic tower episode in the third day's trial, for they consist of a trap and an evasion. Many critics have suggested that in the tower scene, Satan prepares a trap, and the interpretation of Dick Taylor, Jr., is basically correct: Satan asks Jesus to do either of what would seem to be the only two alternatives—to stand miraculously or to fall; Jesus escapes by refusing both the alternatives.[18] So subtle is Milton's rendering that critics have missed the earlier trap. Satan asks permission to return, and covers in his opening concession what would seem to be the only alternative to permission: "From thee I can and must submiss endure/ Check or reproof" (1. 476–77). The alternatives constitute a trap, for, as will

be shown, permission would be an act of impiety, and refusal an act
of injustice. Jesus avoids the trap by accepting neither alternative: "I
bid not or forbid" (1. 495). The escape is as quiet as the trap.

Each of the sets of speeches in the first day's trial concentrates on
a different faculty, then; but each also incorporates elements relating
to all the faculties of the soul: every trial is a complete one. The sensory
element in Satan's opening attack is the temptation to eat in excess
of need. Satan disguises indulgence here with the argument that the
bread eaten would be no more than what is needful, that Jesus would
be "sav[ing] [him]self" (1. 344). Satan also tries to enhance sensory
goods, stimulating love of food with his description of the meager diet
of desert-dwellers and of the hunger and thirst of unwary desert travelers (1. 338–40, 323–25). In the following two speeches, Satan approaches appetite obliquely: instead of asking Jesus to eat, he asks that
Jesus approve the request to eat, and, in so doing, both retract his
earlier refusal and condone intemperance. The confutation with which
Satan closes his second speech, his denial that envy leads him to seek
men's ruin, ends with the words, "This wounds me most . . . that
man,/ Man fall'n, shall be restored, I never more." Jesus' retort is his
reference to these words: "Deservedly thou griev'st, composed of lies/
From the beginning" (1. 407–8). Since Satan ends by sidling up to
Jesus, and since he is lying, the point in his denial of enmity to man
must be to defend the interest he previously expressed in Jesus' health
and comfort: he is falsely claiming that he has no ulterior reason to
seek Jesus' destruction, and is in fact a neglected admirer of Jesus.
When rebuffed, Satan replies with a subtler version of the same argument. In the concession with which he opens his third speech, he
argues that his lies are venial sins, "wrested from [him]" not by "will/
But misery" (1. 468–74); he claims that his request to Jesus was,
though not innocent, at least excusable. Here the appeal to appetite
is made triply subtle: Jesus would yield to what is already a subtle
transgression against temperance not by eating or even by approving
the request to eat, but merely by failing to condemn the request to
a sufficient degree. In addition, Satan exemplifies intemperance in
these two arguments. In the earlier, he fallaciously claims temperance.
Citing his knowledge that he cannot lessen his pain by causing pain
to others and his knowledge that his actions are damnable—knowledge which could provide a basis for the restraint of envy—Satan
falsely claims that therefore he has ceased to be envious. The falsehood is clear from the fact that Satan is indirectly claiming not to be
the foe of Jesus, whom he envies (1. 38). The fact is that, enslaved to

his passions, Satan cannot curb his envy no matter how futile or self-destructive he knows it to be. In the later speech, Satan excuses intemperance, equating his constant malice with incidental weakness. If Jesus does not act evilly, at least he may approve passional evil—so Satan hopes—by mistaking the theoretical grounds of temperance for the achieved virtue, or by mistaking for a forgivable sin hardened intemperance.

The trial of reason in Satan's opening speech is his appeal for charity. By introducing himself as a distant desert-dweller whom "fame" nevertheless "finds . . . out" (1. 330–34), Satan tempts Jesus to a self-aggrandizing act of bounty for an unexpected admirer; and by seeking "food" as a "wretched" beggar (1. 345), he asks Jesus to distribute doles like a Roman emperor, in pursuit of worldly power. The central argument in Satan's second speech, his proof of friendship to man, answers Jesus' rejection of Satan as his subject. In reply to Jesus' rebuke for flattery ("I discern thee other than thou seem'st"), Satan claims to be an influential friend of man, man's "Copartner" and "disposer" (1. 387–93); he thereby answers the suggestion that his earlier admirer's pose was misleading, tempts Jesus to accept a follower flatteringly important, and offers aid in the pursuit of such self-interested goals as Satan himself has pursued. In reply to Jesus' scorn of "bread alone" (1. 347, 349–51), Satan claims to be, through his oracles, a spiritual guide (1. 393–96); he also offers by implication to assist Jesus in the spiritual care he has preferred to material doles, and tempts him to substitute control for instruction. The end of the opening concession in Satan's last speech (1. 475–78) refers to Jesus' words on the subject of oracles. By his fawning acceptance of "Check or reproof," Satan implies that Jesus in rebuking Satan has already accepted him as a follower, demanding subservience from him in a self-interested exercise of authority. "[T]hou art placed above me, thou art Lord" is Satan's reply to Jesus' identification of himself as the "living Oracle" who will supercede Satan's oracles; Satan twists the announcement of a teacher's mission into a declaration of ordinary kingly sovereignty. In addition, by claiming that though Jesus did not grant his flattering appeal for food, he did commit equivalent sins, Satan sets up a retort to the rejection which Jesus might give to his request to return: should Jesus reject the request, Satan could construe the refusal as a self-aggrandizing "reproof" or a claim of "Lord[ly]" sovereignty.

In his opening speech, Satan tries Jesus' intellect with his request for a miracle. His opening reference to Jesus' baptism (1. 326–30) tempts Jesus to show pride in his holiness; Satan mentions the honor done to Jesus, and by expressing doubt ("thou seem'st the man") and surprise ("I ask . . . and the more admire"), he challenges Jesus to demonstrate his worth. The request proper (1. 342–43) is, as Jesus' reply suggests, an invitation to "distrust," a doubt of God's word which is a doubt of his divinity: the opening clause, "if thou be the Son of God," tempts Jesus to seek proof of what he should accept on faith. In his second speech, Satan defends his earlier statements, opening with a concession which replies to Jesus' closing thrust, "I know who thou art." Satan's claim that he has permission to leave hell (1. 358–67) is applied in the later summary when Satan defends his desire to "see" and "approach" Jesus and "hear attent" his "wisdom" (1. 383–86): he is justifying his attendance at the baptism, claiming that he can piously seek out the Son of God. Satan's second argument, that he does God's bidding because he still "admire[s]" whatever he "see[s] excellent in good, or fair,/ Or virtuous" (1. 368–82), is applied in the summary when Satan defends his desire to "behold" Jesus' "godlike deeds" (1. 386): here of course Satan is defending his request to see a miracle. Should Jesus admit that Satan was justified in his conduct, he would be approving the vain and distrustful suggestions. Furthermore, Satan's replies rely on a fallacious claim of piety. By a cunning self-correction (epanorthosis), Satan equates the theoretical recognition of holiness with actual piety; claiming that he has not ceased "To love, at least contemplate and admire" excellence (1. 379–80), he implies that the distinction between recognition and pious response is a minor one—a matter of rephrasing, merely. By suggesting that he loves God, Satan can use his physical actions, his appearance in heaven and his performance of God's bidding, as evidence of a holy spiritual state. If Jesus accepted the argument, he would be mistaking the absence of piety for piety. In his third speech, Satan not only answers Jesus' rebuttal to his assertions, but slyly sums up his two previous assaults. In the first part of the proposal with which he closes his third speech ("Hard are the ways of truth" [1. 477–85]), Satan, proclaiming his "delight" in hearing truth's "dictates from [Jesus'] mouth," repeats the desire he expressed in his second speech to hear Jesus' words. When he concedes that he "despair[s] to attain" virtue, he meets Jesus' disproof of his supposedly innocent interest, and at the same time he renovates the incitement to vanity from his first speech: he asks Jesus to demonstrate his piety for a humble disciple. In the second part of the proposal, in which Satan argues that his request to return is justified by God's treatment of impious priests and prophets (1. 486–92), Satan turns any permission which Jesus might give him into a display of divinity like the distrustful miracle. In addition, by comparing himself to priests and prophets, Satan repeats what he claimed in his second speech about his obedience to God; the comparison to *impious* priests makes an undamaging concession to Jesus' rebuttal. The proposal also contains a reworking of Satan's pretense of piety. When Satan likens himself to ordinary men who "admire/ Virtue" but "follow not her lore," he equates hardened impiety with venial frailty, trying again to win Jesus' condonation.

Jesus' reference to Moses and Elijah (1. 351–54) is his reply to Satan's initial trial of the sensory faculty. Satan's fallacious suggestion that the bread he urges Jesus to eat would not be excessive is answered by Jesus' citation of men whose lives were not endangered by forty day fasts. Furthermore, when Jesus says that Moses "nor eat nor drank," he refers to Satan's description of the desert travelers "pined with hunger and with drouth," and when he says that Elijah lived in the "barren waste," he refers to Satan's description of the "roots and stubs" on which desert-dwellers subsist: so much for Satan's attempt to enhance food. In the following two replies, Jesus turns back Satan's oblique assaults. Satan's elaborate defense of himself, based on his cessation of envy, is answered by Jesus in a parenthesis on the way to his first main argument. In saying "Deservedly thou griev'st, composed of lies/ From the beginning, and in lies wilt end," Jesus denies that Satan is a neglected admirer: approving the fact that Satan will not be "restored," Jesus rejects his claim of good intentions. At the same time he denies Satan's false claim of temperate self-control. Another terse parenthesis—"I know thy scope" (1. 494)—answers Satan's subsequent extenuation of his lying. Jesus points out the malicious motives which disprove both Satan's claim that his request to Jesus was an understandable deception and Satan's pretense that he is only a minor sinner.

Jesus' definition of just rule in his pronouncement concerning oracles is anticipated in his rebuff to Satan's opening appeal for charity. Jesus' rejection of bread for the "word/ Proceeding from the mouth of God" (1. 349–50) prepares for his later definition of rule as the guidance of the inner man. Jesus' attack on Satan's hypocritical flattery ("I discern thee") parallels his later characterization of Satan as God's "fawning parasite" (1. 444–53), the characterization with which he meets Satan's claim to be man's "Copartner" and "disposer." Jesus sees that Satan is trying at this point to make him a self-interested ruler, for he here exposes Satan's self-interest, his "ascri[ption]" to himself of the "truth foretold" by God. Jesus' opening citation of Deuteronomy [19] — his reference to the Jews murmuring for their bread in the wilderness — parallels his later reference to the "Idolatrous" nations which are the prey of Satan's delusive oracles (1. 432–44); the physical control which Satan proposes first is like the delusive mental control which he proposes later, a domination over corrupt men which is opposed to the enlightenment Jesus aims at. Jesus' final speech serves to deny Satan's aspersions on his justice, as well as to evade the trap which Satan has prepared. By saying that he does not forbid Satan's return, Jesus refutes the claim that he has given Satan a self-aggrandizing and lordly rebuke, and prevents Satan from using a refusal to support the charge.

Jesus' demonstration of holiness in the opening exchange parallels his demonstration of justice. As Jesus identified Satan as an enemy of justice, using the discrepancy between his praise of Jesus' fame and his request for bread, so he identifies Satan as an enemy of holiness by the discrepancy between his description of the baptism and his request for a distrustful miracle; and as Jesus attacked in passing Satan's proposal of self-interested rule, so he subordinates the attack on vanity to the rejection of misbelief, "distrust." In his second speech, Jesus rejects Satan's defenses of his initial temptation. Jesus' first argument (1. 409–20) is his "imaginative re-creation" of Satan's feeling of unholiness when in heaven — the reading is Barbara Lewalski's; [20] his second (1. 421–28) is the naming of Satan's impious reasons for obeying God's commands.

These arguments dispose of Satan's two proofs of his innocent interest in the Son of God, and at the end Jesus connects these proofs with Satan's opening temptation: "For lying is thy sustenance, thy food" (1. 429). Jesus pointedly refers to Satan's request to see a miraculous trnsformation: Satan has no need for the bread, he suggests — the deceitful request was sustenance enough. In addition, by dwelling on Satan's feelings and motives, Jesus exposes the fallacy in Satan's use of his external actions as evidences of his holiness. Jesus in his final speech refuses to glorify himself or to test his divinity; instead of asserting his own powers, he tells Satan to act "as [he] find[s]/ Permission from above." His statement that he "bid[s] not" Satan's return also serves to reject Satan's sophistical pieties and his pretense that he is an imperfect seeker after holiness: in failing to grant Satan's request, Jesus refuses to credit his poses.

3

The Evening and the Morning
of the Second Day

THE BANQUET and the offer of learning bear the same relation to the second day's trial that Satan's confession of his identity and his later request to return bear to the first day's trial: they are the second day's analogues to the other days' trials. The banquet tests whether the just man will abandon justice for appetitive satisfaction, the offer of learning whether he will abandon it for intellectual satisfaction.

Elizabeth Pope, arguing that the banquet is not part of the temptation of kingdoms, notes its differences from the "other glories of the world," that "The feast is not associated with any particular realm, nor is it in any way related to the winning or exercise of purely human and temporal sovereignty." [1] These differences also apply to the offer of learning, for Satan's statement that Jesus may study in Athens "or as [he] lik[es], at home" (4. 281) divorces that offer from a particular kingdom, while his statement that he will no longer "Advise" Jesus about the "kingdoms of the world" (4. 209–10) separates the offer from the earlier political instructions.

These details only emphasize the oddity of the attachment of offers of food and education to the subject of kingdoms. The banquet and offer of learning are differentiated in this way because they are thematically different from the other offers; but the banquet scene is not removed from the temptation of kingdoms, as Miss Pope suggests, nor is the offer of learning. Belial's proposal that Satan "Set women in [Jesus'] eye and in his walk" (2. 153–71) has the function of generalizing the opening trial of the flesh: Satan's rejection of the proposal implies that the kind of moral qualities demonstrated in Jesus' imperviousness to gluttony applies to the control of other appetites as well. But in addition, the close of Satan's rejection, "Therefore with manlier objects we must try/ His constancy" (2. 225–30), serves to introduce a change of faculties: it differentiates the coming series of trials from the past test of the sensory soul, making explicit the division implied by the set of introductions interposed between the days. The final summary with which Satan ends the second day's trial ("Since neither wealth, nor honor, arms nor arts" [4. 368–72]) has the similar function of announcing the end of a series of tests, differentiating the offer of learning which anticipates the third day's trial from the third day itself.

The banquet and offer of learning are separated not only from the other days' trials, but also from the rest of the temptations of the second day. When Barbara Lewalski considers the banquet episode as part of the subject of Jesus' kingship, she groups it with the offers of wealth and glory; [2] her argument that Satan seems "not to be seriously discomfited" by Jesus' refusal, that he is more dismayed by the refusals of the next two offers [3] supports her division of the material by emphasizing the continuity between the three offers. In the later cases, however, Milton contents himself with unemphatic transitions: "Satan stood a while as mute" (3. 1–2), "here again/ Satan had not answer" (3. 145–46). The banquet scene not only ends with a striking action, the removal of the banquet by demons, but ends with what is a striking psychological occurrence, Satan's exposure of his evil motives; the transition serves to place an emphatic break after the episode. Northrop Frye, who groups the offer of learning with the offers of Parthia and Rome, as "temptations to false heroic action," [4] misses the events which place structural punctuation after the offer of Rome. Satan's announcement of the price for the kingdoms is an outburst of anger at the failure of all his baits,[5] and afterward Satan is forced to rethink his position. The transitional statement, "Therefore let pass, as they are transitory,/ The kingdoms of this world" (4. 209–10), divorces the coming offer from the past ones; and the reference to Jesus' early history (Jesus' disputation with the rabbis [4. 215–21]) shows Satan's hunt for a clue to some new approach.

In his offer of learning, Satan offers not one kind of learning but three—poetry, oratory, and philosophy; the three varieties correlate with the three faculties of the soul. The temptations made in the offers proper (4. 254–84) are subtly supplemented by suggestions in the introduction (4. 221–53); this section, which compares the contemplative to the heroic life, invites Jesus to a self-directed use of the faculties. The opening two arguments (4. 221–28, 229–35) are flanked by a military metaphor: Satan begins by comparing learning to world conquest—"as thy empire must extend,/ So let extend thy mind o'er all the world"—and he ends by comparing argumentative to military victory—"Error by his own arms is best evinced." The exhortations in between have military overtones: Satan argues that all knowledge is not contained in the Bible as if he were urging a parochial Jewish king to look beyond his borders, and he praises the gentiles' knowledge as if it were fertile and conquerable foreign land; he asks Jesus how he can meet the gentiles on unequal terms or refute their arguments, as if arguments were armaments. The final section of the introduction (4. 236–53) is a description of the beauties of Athens, but it ends with a reminder that the scene is not an unsuitable one for heroes: Satan identifies the Lyceum by its connection with Alexander, and what Satan calls the "painted Stoa" was painted with scenes from the Trojan war. The first argument tempts Jesus to glory in learning, and the image recalls Jesus' earlier exemplification of spiritual vanity in the person of the "unpraised" warrior Scipio (3. 100–107). The second argument explicitly recognizes Jesus' intention to "rul[e] . . . by persuasion," but seeks to turn this aim to self-interested ends; Satan tries to interest Jesus in the pleasure of winning arguments and to threaten him with the disgrace of losing them. The description of Athens is an invitation to self-indulgence. The temptation to eat to excess is subordinated to the temptation to seek a physical comfort which contrasts with the rigors of the wilderness—though Satan does not neglect to choose for his background olive groves, honey-making insects, and streams. The excess is cloaked by the moralizing reference to the "industrious murmur" of the bees, conducive to "studious musing," and by the final heroic references, whose point is their suggestion that ease is not debilitating.

The offers of learning themselves tempt Jesus to direct his faculties to improper ends. The offer of philosophic learning (4. 272–80) is a temptation to misbelief: Satan asks Jesus to suspend faith for the contemplation of a variety of metaphysical systems, none of them based on divine revelation. The personification of philosophy as a goddess descending to Socrates' humble roof has been compared (misleadingly) to Cicero's praise of Socrates for turning philosophy from metaphysics to ethics,[6] and Satan's comparison of Socrates to a spring which feeds a branching river has been compared to Quintillian's tribute to Socrates' influence;[7] but there is more dramatic point in taking these metaphors as allusions to familiar biblical texts. In Proverbs wisdom is personified as a goddess who descends to the city and calls men to "Receive [her] instruction, and not silver," and Proverbs compares the words of the wise to a spring: [8] Satan is giving religious sanction to the nonreligious study he proposes. The second branch of learning offered, oratory (4.267–71, is a temptation to power. Satan again makes an explicit appeal to Jesus' idea of rule; by referring to "democraty" he recognizes Jesus' intention to govern by persuasion rather than by force. In this case Satan tries to replace instruction with manipulation. In a metaphor whose point is its enhancement of power, he likens the orator to Jove and his followers to weapons: the orator "wield[s]" the "fierce" horses of the state, he "Sh[akes] the Arsenal" like a spear,[9] he "fulmine[s] over Greece" with a divine thunder. Satan's remaining offer, that of poetry (4. 254–66), tempts Jesus' sensory soul. Emotive impact is what Satan emphasizes, the "secret power/ Of harmony in tones and numbers hit/ By voice or hand, and various-measured verse"; and he repeatedly returns to the formal allurements of meter and music, "charms" and "odes," "chorus" and "iambic" being metrical distinctions, and the "poem Phoebus challenged for his own" a reminder of music. Satan meets the Platonic objection to such sensory distractions by arguing, on the basis of one genre, that poetry encourages virtue instead of corrupting it; but even here he is careful to make poetic content an emotional stimulus, reducing morality to that pleasant figure *sententia:* "teachers . . . with delight received/ In brief sententious precepts."

Jesus replies to Satan's sensory temptations with distinctions between excessive and rightful leisure and between harmful and permissible pleasures. He temperately refuses Athens in the summer, content with spare time at home (4. 331–34). By likening pagan poets and poetry to drunken singers and painted harlots, Jesus notes Satan's appeal to appetite, and he dismisses Satan's glorification of sensory beauty with a Platonic attack on the corrupting content of poetry. Though he concedes the validity of Satan's moral defense, he attacks Satan's sophistical overextension of it (4. 334–52). In addition, Jesus restores his idea of rule after Satan's distortions. He describes guidance as the propagation of simple truths, rather than as argumentative warfare (4. 361–63), and he endorses the pious prophets' instructions rather than the orator's seizures of godlike control (4. 353–60).

But Jesus gives his most elaborate rebuttal to Satan's intellectual assaults. Contrasting holiness with pride in knowledge, he uses the metaphor of digestion to discuss the assimilation of learning, and chooses two forms of sickness, indigestion and drunkenness, to represent the two forms of educational vanity, pedantry and snobbishness (4. 321–30). Jesus also contrasts faith with metaphysical speculation, arguing that revelation is the only necessary knowledge and that philosophizing which departs from it is error (4. 286–321). Each of these arguments he heads with an allusion, one to the words of Solomon, the other to the words of David; [10] the two men exemplify holy wisdom as contrasted with vain or godless learning.

Each of the arguments he closes with a striking image which answers the metaphors Satan has used to tempt him. Satan compares the learned man to a hero, Jesus compares him to a child; Satan compares wide learning to conquerable kingdoms, Jesus compares it to gathered pebbles. In reply to Satan's personification of philosophy as a goddess visiting the humble, Jesus likens philosophic wisdom to the simulacrum loved by pampered Ixion; and through their suggestions of rainlessness, the words which describe the mock Hera, "empty cloud," also glance at the comparison of Socrates' wisdom to a fertile stream. The unexpected mythological reference answers Satan's biblical allusions: if Satan can give biblical sanction to impiety, Jesus can give pagan sanction to piety.

Satan's main lure in this trial is intellectual, and his aim is to distract Jesus from his ruler's duties. In the transition which precedes the temptation, Satan suggests that Jesus is a contemplative rather than an active type: "Thou thyself seem'st otherwise inclined/ Than to a worldly crown, addicted more/ To contemplation and profound dispute" (4. 212–14). Satan's final summary shows his intention of turning Jesus away from kingdom:

> These [studies] here revolve, or as thou lik'st, at home,
> Till time mature thee to a kingdom's weight;
> These rules will render thee a king complete
> Within thyself, much more with empire joined.
>   (4. 281–84)

The lines refer to Jesus' earlier pious resolve to wait for God's time and to his central definition of temperance, as well as to his predicted kingship. They refer therefore to all three faculties, but what is significant is the choice and weight: contemplation is a good holy activity — especially when it delays kingship; contemplation will perfect Jesus' temperance, and temperance is a good quality for a king — if kingdom should happen to come Jesus' way. The aim of distracting Jesus explains the way in which Satan discusses governing, for in addition to making the obligatory attempts to pervert Jesus' rule, Satan proposes delay.

He begins by making the persuasive use of learning a secondary advantage to the primary aim of attaining universal knowledge, and he continues by putting the study of the techniques of controlling men in the place of rule itself. The explicit references which Satan makes to Jesus' definition of rule function as sops, assurances that Jesus is pursuing what Satan hopes he will neglect. The diversionary tactic also shows in the organizational devices of Satan's speech. The reason that the introductory section is built around a metaphor comparing contemplative activities to kingly ones is that Satan hopes to put study in the place of rule. The offer of the branches of learning is organized temporally rather than simply numerically: "Thence to the famous orators repair (4. 267), "To sage philosophy next lend thine ear" (4. 272). The suggestion is that rational oratory is merely a step on the way to intellectual philosophy.

Jesus sees and replies to this attempt to distract him. His speech, like Satan's proposal, is structured around the three branches of knowledge, but whereas Satan adopts the logical climactic order, Jesus chooses not the equally logical anticlimactic order, but an illogical sequence which ends with the rational field, government, rather than the sensory one, poetry. Thus though Jesus places major emphasis on Satan's central, intellectual appeal, he puts the question of rule in the important ending position, to show that he has not forgotten it; and he ends with a jab at Satan's closing minimization of kingship: "These only [the prophets] with our Law best form a king" (4. 364).

The tripartite pattern which runs throughout *Paradise Regained* is present in the banquet episode not only in the debate but in the description of the banquet itself. The comparison of the "cates" proffered Jesus to the "crude apple that diverted Eve" (2. 348–49) establishes the appetitive element in the feast. "[D]iverted" in the sense of "entertain" points to the self-indulgence involved, while the lack of simplicity described indicates that the banquet is meant to produce an absorption with the senses. "[D]iverted" in the sense of "turn aside from his course" not only judges the transgression but, by its comparison of Eve to Atalante, prepares for the appetitive appeals of wealth in the later attempts. The significance of the description of the meats and fowl and of the fish fetched from "Pontus and Lucrine bay, and Afric coast" (2. 337–47) is pointed to by the heading, "A table richly spread, in regal mode." The banquet tempts Jesus to the sort of self-interested rule that is implied by the regal tribute, and to the sort of power over men that is implied by the ability to gather the exotic delicacies.

Though the attendants of the banquet are often interpreted as Mrs. Lewalski interprets them, as "one of the elements in [a] panorama of refined sensual pleasure," [11] the trappings are described in a way suggestive of religious temptation. The deities (2. 350–56) are dichotomized into deities of air and those of water. Ganymede was carried into the heavens, Hylas into the waters; Diana's nymphs serve a heavenly goddess, while the Naiades are water nymphs. The last attendants, "the ladies of th' Hesperides," are compared to the "fairy damsels" met by Lancelot, Pelleas, and "Pellenore"; these also fall into two classes. Mrs. Lewalski is right in suggesting that "Pellenore" actually refers to Pellenore's son, Percivale.[12] His temptress is identified with the sky, for she is finally revealed as the "master fiend of hell" whom "our Lord Jesus Christ beat him out of heaven for his sin," and she is earlier linked with air by way of allusion to Satan's title, Prince of the Air: her ship came "as all the wind of the world had driven it," her pavilion turned to "a smoke and a black cloud," and she left "with the wind roaring and yelling that it seemed all the water burnt after her." [13]

Mrs. Lewalski is mistaken in identifying the allusions to Lancelot and Pelleas, however. The lines refer to the knights' association with "fairy damsels," while the women she names, Elaine and Ettard,[14] are ordinary mortal women. The fairy that Lancelot met was Morgan le Fay, while Pelleas became the lover of the sorceress Nynyve.[15] The knights are paired in that one resisted while the other embraced a water deity: Nynyve is the Lady of the Lake, and Morgan is one of the three queens who attended her when she carried off Arthur's body.[16] The setting of the banquet (2. 262–65) is also dichotomized, into airy and earthy constituents. The music comes from "chiming strings," the lyre of heavenly Apollo, and from "charming pipes," the pipes of earthly Pan; the scent consists of "Arabian odors," smells associated with the winds, and of "Flora's earliest smells," the smells of earth.

Together the two sets of dichotomies suggest the dichotomy of heaven and earth: water can stand for earth because it is the terrestrial realm of Poseidon as contrasted with the heavenly realm of Zeus. Thus the trappings are made to recall God's title, the Lord of Heaven and Earth; but heaven and earth are defined in a naturalistic way, as the sky and the surface of the world. Furthermore, the attendants are grouped in a way suggestive of the two ways in which holiness may be violated. Diana's nymphs and Ganymede are servants, and there-fore the Naiades and Hylas, paired with them, must be servants too; they represent the temptation to self-interest, vanity. The Hesperides are identified by their beauty and are linked with seductresses: they are thereby separated from the servants. The fact that they were un-faithful guardians of Hera's apples suggests that they represent the temptation to conceive of nature in isolation from God; and the com-plementary aspect of this sort of heresy, the idea that God does not care about humanity, is suggested by the opposition between the seductresses and Christ's role as bridegroom, a role which asserts God's love for men. This group of attendants, then, is made to symbol-ize the heretical acceptance of materialism.

Satan's opening speech (2. 302–16) is a jaunty revision of the appeti-tive attack with which he opened the first day's trial. By analogy to his initial "Sir, what ill chance hath brought thee to this place" (1. 321), Satan describes Jesus as "destitute" in the "wild solitude," and by analogy to his initial restatement, "we here/ Live on tough roots and stubs" (1. 338–39), Satan closes with another reference to the wilder-ness, "Forty [days] and more deserted here indeed." The main part of the speech corresponds to the main part of the first temptation; it is an argument that Jesus would save his life by eating, rebutting Jesus' citation of Moses and Elijah (1. 351–54). Satan suggests that God does not "support" life "without repast," as Jesus has thought (2. 250): he notes that God supplied food to Ishmael and the Israelites, and implies that these cases prove that what sustained Elijah was the two meals God provided him.

This main attack is an attack on Jesus' resolve to "fear no harm" from the "sting of famine" (2. 257), but Satan's pun, "deserted here indeed," suggests that the opening is a light one, designed to get Jesus to repeat his former answer, so that Satan can reply with his convincing retort, "How hast thou hunger then?" (2. 319). This challenge tallies with Jesus' own observation that "Nature hath need of what she asks" (2. 252–53), and its fallacy is not its internal weakness but its inapplica-bility to the banquet Satan has prepared: that banquet exceeds mere need, and therefore tempts Jesus to violate his resolve to be content so long as his body does not waste (2. 254–56). The banquet by its showiness also picks up Satan's opening hint about the desolate desert, and tempts Jesus to forget those "better thoughts" which keep him from "mind[ing]" the "sting of famine" (2. 258–59).

When Satan asks him if he would not eat, Jesus replies, "Thereafter as I like/ The giver (2. 321–22). To take this as a flat rejection of anything offered by Satan is to remove the rational combat, the test of reason by sophistry. The alternative is to view the statement as a piece of political prudence: gifts involve obligations. Jesus is citing Proverbs: "When thou sittest to eat with a ruler, consider diligently what is before thee. . . . Be not desirous of his dainties, for they are deceitful meat." [17] Satan answers this political argument in the parenthetical concession which forms the center section of his second main speech (2. 327–31). The subject of the concession is dining with rulers. Satan's reference to Nebuchadnezzar's gathering of the noble children of the Israelites is a claim of worldly sovereignty and an attempt to make a protégé of Jesus. Satan's disclaimers attempt to prove that the relationship is innocent, by distinguishing Jesus' case from Daniel's: Satan is not a conqueror of Israel, "an enemy," and he is not offering food from a Babylonian king's table, "Meats . . . unclean" and "offered first/ To idols." The former argument restates the claim Satan made in his second speech in the first day's trial, that he is mankind's friend; the qualification, that no one "with want oppressed" would "scruple" to take food from an enemy, answers Jesus' objection to the claim of friendship (1. 444–53). The other argument answers Jesus' statement that God gave "the nations up" to Satan's "delusions" because they "fell/ Idolatrous" (1. 432–44): Satan dissociates himself from heathen customs. In the first case, Satan is asking Jesus to accept the fruits of worldly power on the basis of need, and therefore for self-interested motives. In the second he is generalizing, falsely, on the basis of a particular example of lawfulness.

The main test of the intellect is Satan's exhortation after the presentation of the banquet (2. 368–77). Here the argument is built around a reference to the first Adam; "these are Spirits of air, and woods, and springs,/ Thy gentle ministers" alludes to Adam's sovereignty over fowl, beasts, and fish, and "These are not fruits forbidden" of course alludes to God's prohibition. These references conceal the religious issues in the way that Satan's references to Daniel conceal the political ones, and the fallacies in the arguments parallel those in the lower test. The argument that Jesus deserves the servants' tributes dodges the question of vain self-display, and the argument about the interdiction conceals a general transgression under the denial of a specific narrower transgression: nature is being offered in isolation from God even if not in contradiction to God's prohibition.

The suggestion that Satan tests Jesus through a violation of the Mosaic dietary laws does not add to the sublimity of this episode, and the theory—offered by Michael Fixler and accepted by Mrs. Lewalski

—is not a probable one. The main objection is that the issue which these critics raise, that of the abrogation of the Law, is not raised in the poem. The reasons which they give for the absence are not convincing. Fixler says that it "would have been incongruous for the Savior to argue the point of ritual purity with Satan," [18] and Mrs. Lewalski says that Jesus escapes the dilemma of accepting either idolatry or the "bondage of the law" by refusing the banquet on extraneous grounds.[19]

Both of these explanations show Jesus weakly dodging the rational problem posed for him, and neither explanation tells why if the issue of the Mosaic law is in fact present, Jesus could not observe as succinctly as Fixler that "the food really was pure and clean, but not for the reason Satan offered." [20] A second objection is that the vague reason Mrs. Lewalski assigns Satan—that he expects to "confuse" Jesus "with . . . theological complexities" [21]—cannot make plausible what would have been a foolish maneuver on Satan's part. If Satan lies when he claims that the "Meats" are not "by the Law unclean" and that "no interdict/ Defends the touching" of the "viands pure," he gives Jesus easy factual rebuttals to what would otherwise be subtle logical problems. The evidence, furthermore, that the food at the banquet is "manifestly unclean" (as Fixler puts it) [22] is not so striking that one may not conclude that when Milton described the Roman royal banquet, he slipped on a detail of Mosaic law. Mrs. Lewalski says that the banquet "probably" contains "some forbidden flesh," [23] but Milton does not call attention to any violation: he says "meats of noblest sort . . . beasts of chase, or fowl of game," when he could have named bear's head and breast of swan. One forbidden food which Fixler lists is ambergris,[24] but this violation is not one which is obvious from the regulations given in the eleventh chapter of Leviticus. Shellfish is the one clear violation, but Milton's description suggests that his point is the opulence of the banquet, not any illegitimacy in its contents: "all fish from sea or shore . . . of shell or fin,/ And exquisitest name, for which was drained/ Pontus and Lucrine bay, and Afric coast." Mrs. Lewalski says that the banquet "admittedly contains forbidden shellfish and grisamber," [25] but she does not notice that the admission is Milton's, not Satan's, and does not consider that the trial she places upon Jesus is not his knowledge of the Law, therefore, but his knowledge of cooking. Assuming that there is a sin in not knowing or not following the biblical regulations concerning ambergris, would Jesus be condemned if he failed to recognize by smell an ingredient that no good Jewish boy is supposed to know?

Jesus replies to Satan's opening jaunty speech with a jaunty speech of his own: Ishmael, the Israelites, and Elijah, he says, "all had need [of food], I as thou seest have none" (2. 318). "[A]s thou seest" refers to the wilderness, whose emptiness Jesus wittily makes a metaphor for his lack of need, answering at once the argument that he would be saving his life and the solicitation that, "deserted," he dream of food. In his final speech, Jesus answers Satan's retort, pointing to the qualities of the banquet which refute Satan's argument; "pompous delicacies" (2. 390) succinctly notes both the excess ("pompous") and the sensuousness ("delicacies") in the provisions. Jesus' statement that he "count[s]" Satan's "specious gifts" as "guiles" (2. 391) repeats the political prudence of "as I like/ The giver," and paraphrases the text which Jesus had cited earlier: "Be not desirous of [a ruler's] dainties, for they are deceitful meat." "Guiles" accuses Satan of attempting to corrupt Jesus; "gifts" suggests the appeal to self-interest, and "specious" denies the claim of lawfulness which Satan has made (for though the meats of the banquet may be legally clean, as he says, they stand for a kind of external power which is contrary to Jesus' spiritual guidance).

Jesus answers Satan's attack on the intellect with a reply (2. 379–88) that is distinctive not only for its length but for the virtuosity in its manipulation of the materials Satan has supplied. In preferring angels to Satan's "Spirits of air, and woods, and springs," and in preferring God's "table" to Satan's "viands pure," Jesus is opposing servants and food that represent nature in the governance of God to those that represent nature in isolation from him. But in rejecting Satan's offer Jesus comes tantalizingly close to doing all that Satan asks and more. Tempted to vain self-display, he lays claim not only to the service of spirits but to the banquet as well (2. 283–86). Tempted to materialistic heresy, Jesus not only claims Satan's fruits but the servants to present them (2. 279–82). Yet, by paradox, these acceptances avoid the moral snares which Satan has laid. Jesus' boast is not vain because it is a tribute to the glory of God: "I can . . . Command a table in the wilderness" reverses the cry of the impious in the psalm, who doubted God's power to "furnish a table in the wilderness," and "I can . . . call swift flights of angels" affirms the faith of the man who finds, the psalm says, "refuge" and "fortress" in God, and over whom God "shall give his angels charge . . . to keep [him] in all [his] ways." [26] Jesus' claim to the "viands" is not an affirmation of materialism because it is a statement of belief in the Sonship God has declared ("Shall I receive by gift what of my own . . . I can command?"); the claim thus rejects distrust (the point here is like that in Jesus' refusal to test God's pronouncement with a miraculous transformation of stones). Jesus claims divinity by glorifying God and glorifies God by claiming divinity, and in so doing he demonstrates humble faith.

An oddity noted by Miss Pope suggests that Satan's strategy in the banquet episode is similar to his strategy in the offer of learning. The oddity is that in an offer which deals with justice primarily (or with temperance, Miss Pope believes), the issue of godhood is "the one issue which is fought at any length." [27] Miss Pope argues, rightly, that Satan's aim is revealed in the transition with which he begins the following offer, though she does not notice that at that point Satan does not merely pay tribute to Jesus' temperance, but to temperance as part of Jesus' regal interests: "Thy temperance invincible . . . For no allurement yields to appetite,/ And all thy heart is set on high designs" (2. 408–11). Miss Pope rightly concludes that Satan is using his religious argumentation as a diversionary device,[28] though the diversion is more complicated than she sees: Satan tries to divert Jesus from his "high designs" with appetitive "allurement," and to divert Jesus from this diversion with religious arguments.

This strategy accounts for the organization of Satan's arguments. Satan's main attack is directed against the sensory soul—he is offering food to a hungry man—and he plans from the beginning to use the religious argument as a diversion, for he prepares for it in the first line of his opening speech. "With granted leave officious I return" (2. 302) alludes to the end of the first day's trial and implies that Jesus has already exercised divinity by granting Satan's request to return (Satan conveniently ignores the distinction between permitting and not forbidding); [29] the implication prepares for his later request that the "Son of God . . . sit and eat" (2. 368). That Satan intends the political issue to go unnoticed is suggested by the embarrassed way he handles Jesus' introduction of it. He skirts the issue, reducing his answer to a parenthesis and relying on confutations rather than on positive arguments; the answer is so weak that Jesus can reply with a simple rewording of his original point. In order to bury the unwanted question, Satan flanks his answer with a premature use of his diversionary religious arguments: the opening "Owe not all creatures . . . duty and service" (2. 322–27) anticipates Satan's introduction of the "Spirits of air, and woods, and springs," and the closing "Nature . . . hath purveyed . . . her choicest store" (2. 331–36) anticipates his recommendation of the "viands pure." Presenting the banquet, Satan resumes his plan, speaking only of the peripheral religious issue.

Satan's strategy also accounts for his problematic banquet arrangements. Don Cameron Allen argues that the banquet is overlavish and blames this miscalculation (as he sees it) on Satan's panic after his first day's defeat.[30] Arnold Stein accepts Allen's premise but ingeniously saves Satan's stature; arguing that the banquet "insists on being *wrong,*" he deduces that Satan intends to be "provocative." [31] It *is* tempting to see the refrain which opens and closes Satan's presentation of the banquet as a sarcastic taunt: "What doubts the Son of God"; "What doubt'st thou, Son of God" (2. 368, 377); but Milton's commentary does not allow this construction: "The Tempter . . . His invitation earnestly renewed" (2. 366–67).

But if Satan is not being provocative, he need not be dismissed as foolish, for the lavishness of the banquet can be explained. Though it is true that Satan could have made a less excessive and sensuous temptation to gluttony, Satan hopes not to have to discuss the political aspects of his offer, and therefore he needs a banquet which will constitute in itself an offer of self-interested and worldly sovereignty. A kingly banquet would call attention to itself, however, and therefore Satan camouflages the appetitive and rational transgressions under divine trappings, and devotes an "earnest[ ]" defense to the camouflage.

Satan's loss of temper may be explained by the way in which Jesus meets this artful assault. The length at which Jesus replies to Satan's religious argument suggests that he has indeed been diverted, and the argument he gives tantalizes Satan with its paradoxical near-acceptances. Then Jesus suddenly turns to the main appetitive appeal and to the political argument which Satan is anxious to conceal; he answers each in a single line. The cool elegance of this reproof stings Satan into his petulant outburst.

The Heart of the Offer
of Kingdom

THE FIVE offers in the center of the offer of kingdoms bear the same relation to the second day's trial that the request for bread bears to the first day's trial: they constitute the heart of the temptation. The five are doubly subdivided. Kingdom is offered first as an end entailing the acceptance of a lower, sensory, means; then glory is used as an end and kingdom offered as a means; and finally kingdom is offered for its own sake. But kingdom is presented in several lights. Intellectual and sensory allurements are added to the lure of worldliness before that appeal itself is given full attention.

Rule, the end in the offer of wealth and the means in the offer of glory, is not the primary focus in either episode. In both offers Satan tempts by stimulating rivalry with worldly rulers. First he reminds Jesus that Herod is presently the King of the Jews (2. 424–25), then he asks that Jesus compete with youthful warriors, Alexander and Scipio and Pompey ("Thy years are ripe, and overripe" [3. 31–36]). In the second instance, though Satan gives the date of Pompey's first triumph, he describes the triumph which celebrated a much later campaign, the campaign during which Pompey won Israel: the example enhances the rivalry. In the offer of wealth Satan tempts Jesus to self-interested rule in his parenthetical identification of Herod's realm: "Judah's throne,/ (Thy throne)." His reference to the "puissant friends" who installed Antipater and his son is an inducement to exercise worldly power: Satan suggests that Jesus buy like friends, oust

Herod, and take his place. In the offer of glory Satan argues by models rather than by hints. The appeal for Jesus to assume his throne is replaced by the example of kingdom-seizing Alexander; the suggestion that Jesus expel the Edomite usurper is replaced by the model of Scipio, who drove the Carthaginian invaders from his country.[1] In neither offer is the political argumentation prominent. In the later case the argument is an exhortation to haste subordinate to Satan's main point, the value of glory. In the earlier case Satan moves from the two purchases which he has argued money can buy, "honor" and "friends," to the end for which they are purchased, "conquest" and "realms" (2. 422). Antipater and Herod, buyers of kingdom, serve as instances supporting Satan's central contention, the importance of wealth.

The offers of wealth and glory are complementary in their emphasis, the former emphasizing the lowest faculty, the latter the highest. In both offers the sensory assault is marked by a new object of attack. Turning from what Jesus in his definition of temperance calls "desires" to what he calls "passions" (2. 467), Satan tries to convert Jesus' physical wants into emotional longings. In the offer of wealth he makes Jesus' plight a metaphor for his earlier life, pairing his present hunger with his "straits at home" and his desert surroundings with his "poverty," that is, his obscurity (2. 415–16); he attempts to turn physical deprivation into avarice. In addition Satan links Jesus' plight with the condition of those whom—he argues—Jesus will have to lead. He attributes hunger to these when he claims that Jesus will have to "feed them on [his] cost" (2. 420–21), and when he asks Jesus "Whence" he will derive "authority" (2. 418–19), Satan suggests that men's need for prominence makes them honor only those conspicuous for luxurious display. By this tactic Satan not only connects the acquisition of riches with the acquisition of kingdom, but he tempts Jesus to empathize with and therefore to condone the avarice of others. In the offer of glory, Satan again makes a metaphoric extension of Jesus' physical state, this time an even more drastic extension (3. 37–42). Arguing that years "Quench not the thirst of glory," he makes Jesus' hunger a metaphor for what is not actually a sin of the flesh, the desire for glory. This conversion of pride into passion he continues by comparing Caesar's longing to sexual yearning: Caesar was "inflamed" with glory, he "wept" like a hopeless wooer.

Satan's reference to Jesus' "straits" is an instigation to self-indulgence, and his comment about the anonymity of "poverty" urges Jesus to value the material trappings of royalty. Jesus replies with his definition of temperance (the "ruling" of "Passions, desires, and fears" [2. 465–66]), and Satan tries to evade this definition in his subsequent offer; he argues that the passion for glory is not diminished but "augment[ed]" by "years, and to ripe years judgment mature." The passion which age and maturity lessen is of course sexual passion. Sexual love may violate temperance, Satan implies—people look back on their lustful years with embarassment and shame—but the love of glory is a different sort of passion: no one ever comes to regret *that.* Rebuttal having been made, Satan repeats his earlier temptations. He advises Jesus to indulge the "thirst of glory" as he urged him to make up for lean years; and as he criticized Jesus' obscurity, so he presents him the model of Caesar, who "wept that he had lived so long/ Inglorious." In the offer of wealth the sensory appeal is the main one; "Get riches first, get wealth, and treasure heap," Satan says (2. 427), emphatically summarizing his central point. In the offer of glory, Satan turns the intellectual sin of pride into an emotional sin in order to make the lower temptation an aspect of the higher.

Satan concludes the offer of wealth with an attack on the intellect (3. 428–31). In it, he puts into words the temptations he had exhibited during the banquet.[2] In place of the Hesperidean seductresses (2. 357–61) who represented the temptation to think of nature in isolation from God, Satan presents his argument that "They whom [he] favor[s] thrive in wealth amain,/ While virtue, valor, wisdom, sit in want." Posing as Fortune, he asks Jesus to accept an amoral cause of events in the place of Providence. The issue is made especially clear when Satan boasts his power: "Riches are mine, fortune is in my hand." While paraphrasing a text from Haggai, he appropriates to himself the power of God: "The silver is mine, and the gold is mine, saith the Lord of hosts." [3] In place of the ministering spirits (2. 350–56) who presented the appeal to vain self-assertion, Satan offers his own services: he claims that wealth is "Not difficult" to obtain if Jesus "hearken[s]" to him. Jesus is pressed to make himself the favored of Fortune. The logical function of this intellectual temptation shows it to be a minor element in the offer of wealth. Satan recommends himself as the source of riches in order to prove that his advice to "get wealth" is practical advice. The point is a secondary one.

Satan looks backward in this attack, but in the intellectual assault which opens the offer of glory (3. 7–30) he reaches even further back; he repeats his first day's appeals. Satan ended the first temptation by asking Jesus to imitate the Father, "holy, wise, and pure" (1. 486). Now, calling Jesus "good, wise, just" (the words and order are different, but the qualities are the same), Satan attributes divine sinlessness to Jesus. "I see thou know'st what is of use to know,/ What best to say canst say, to do canst do," he begins, inverting the formula of contrition, "I confess . . . that I have sinned exceedingly in thought, word, and deed." [4] In the center of the first day's trial, Satan defended his desire to "hear" Jesus' "wisdom, and behold [his] godlike deeds" (1. 385–86). Jesus' words and deeds are the subject of the next passage in the offer of glory, and Satan again calls these holy. He likens them to the words of prophets and to the deeds of judges — to the accomplishments of the divinely chosen — and he compares Jesus' counsel to that given by Aaron's "oraculous gems" — to the revelations of God himself. Satan opened the first day with the request for a self-displaying and distrustful miracle. Now, closing this spiritual assault with its point, he advises that Jesus seek glory, and furthermore that he achieve miraculous victories — this last is the meaning of his reproach that Jesus is "depriv[ing]/ All earth her wonder at [his] acts."

Satan's speech of rebuttal, "Think not so slight of glory" (3. 109–20), makes clear that the intellectual temptation is the central one in this offer. The original proposal suggests the reason for the emphasis. Though the temptations Satan uses derive from the first day's trial, he develops them out of motifs in Jesus' refusal of wealth. Satan's praise of Jesus' "wise," "good," and "just" heart stems from the definition of temperance; Jesus attributes the quality to "every wise and virtuous man," and adds that it is a prerequisite for anyone who wishes to "rule/ Cities of men" (2. 468–72). Many editors, glossing Jesus' praise of the refusers of kingdom, supply late classical or modern instances,[5] but these are not dramatically appropriate. Jesus must be thinking of biblical examples. When he speaks of the "lay[ing] down" of kingdom (2. 482), he is thinking of Gideon's rejection of the throne of Israel, and when he says that "giv[ing]" a kingdom has proved nobler than "assum[ing]" one (2. 481–83), he refers to Samuel's anointing of Saul [6] (Samuel's warnings against monarchy were borne out by Saul's career). Satan incorporates these two examples into his praise of Jesus' words and deeds. Comparing Jesus' words to those of "seers old/ Infallible," Satan alludes to Samuel, for whom, the Bible explains, the old word "Seer" was used, not the new word "Prophet." [7] When he claims that "all the world" could not "subsist" against Jesus' "few in arms," Satan alludes to the defeat of the Midianites by Gideon's band of three hundred.[8] Satan closes the recommendation of glory with a description of the pursuers of it, men who, he says, "all pleasures else despise,/ All treasures and all gain esteem as dross,/ And dignities and powers, all but the highest."

The description alludes to the closing words in Jesus' denunciation of money:

> Extol not riches then, the toil of fools,
> The wise man's cumbrance if not snare, more apt
> To slacken virtue and abate her edge
> Than prompt her to do aught may merit praise.
>   (2. 453–56)

Satan elsewhere rebuts particular arguments of Jesus, but the fact that in this one argument Satan draws on motifs gathered from the whole of Jesus' speech shows that something other than counterargument is involved. Satan believes that Jesus' reply has provided him the key to his character, and he thinks that by approaching Jesus on spiritual grounds he can make an appeal to his dominant concerns.

The banquet and offer of learning share a distinctive argumentative strategy, that of distraction. The five offers in the center of the second day are also marked by a common approach, the use of instrumental arguments. The first two offers tender kingdom in terms of something else, and treat the subject of ends and means in a complementary way. In the offer of wealth, emphasis is placed on the means, and the end is used as an excuse. In the offer of glory, emphasis is placed on the end, and the means is justified by reference to it. Jesus in replying shows that he recognizes the tactics. He organizes his answers around means and ends, and refers explicitly both to Satan's methods and to the topics of his own replies: "Riches are needless then, both for themselves,/ And for thy reason why they should be sought,/ To gain a scepter" (2. 484–86), "Thou neither dost persuade me to seek wealth/ For empire's sake, nor empire to affect/ For glory's sake" (3. 44–46).

The opening section of Jesus' rejection of wealth (2. 433–56) is devoted to the subject of money, the means in the offer. In this section Jesus meets Satan's spiritual assault. He rejects on internal grounds Satan's suggestion that he seek to be Fortune's favorite: the move would not advance him, but instead would serve as a confession of weakness ("[W]hat in me seems wanting . . . ?" he asks). By pointedly picking Quintius, Fabricius, Curius, and Regulus as examples of poor men who accomplished "mighty things," Jesus counters with "heathen" examples the pagan world view which Satan invokes. As to Satan's claim that the world is in his hand, that it is ruled by amoral Fortune, Jesus replies in arguing that rich nations have fallen through lack of virtue and virtuous poor men have risen. Embellishing Hannah's praise of providence, "The Lord maketh poor and maketh rich: he bringeth low, and lifteth up . . . for the pillars of the earth are the Lord's, and he hath set the world upon them," Jesus cites Gideon, Jephtha, and David as examples of Hannah's "poor" whom God has "set . . . among princes." [9] He is offering a religious rebuttal to Satan's materialistic metaphysics.

The subject of the second section of Jesus' speech (2. 457–86) is kingdom, the end proposed in the offer of wealth. The four points here —they consist of a concession, two arguments, and a confutation— mingle answers to Satan's rational and passional attacks. In the concession (2. 457–65) and confutation (2. 481–83) Jesus replies to Satan's exhortation that he take the throne of Judah (*his* throne). Maintaining in the concession that the burdens of office are no reason for declining a throne, he upholds kingly self-sacrifice, and asserts a view of governing antithetical to Satan's. In the confutation—the claim that refusing a crown is more kingly than accepting it—he compares disinterestedness to generosity, "giv[ing]" and "lay[ing] down," and glances at Satan's suggestion that the throne is property which the owner should repossess. The second of the section's two arguments—the proof that it is more kingly to teach than to wield worldly power (2. 473–80)— answers the proposal that Jesus govern in Herod's place and in Herod's way. The passage explains in literal terms what the metaphor of the oracle (1. 454–64) had hinted about the nature of Jesus' rule. Satan's sensory assault is treated in the remaining argument, Jesus' contention that self-control is more kingly than control over others (2. 466–72). There Jesus not only answers Satan's temptation to avarice (he offers a plain definition of passional virtue) but he also meets Satan's secondary point, the claim that Jesus will need money in order to attract supporters. When he says that the man who "attains not" temperance "ill aspires to rule/ Cities of men, or headstrong multitudes," he refuses to condone veniality and worldliness. He implies instead that the leader's example should cure the intemperance of his followers.

Jesus' refusal of glory is more complexly organized. The speech contains six points, chiastically ordered, the first three treating the devotion of the faculties to improper ends, the second three the self-interested use of the faculties. The inner points are grouped, however, and as a result, the speech centers around two main subjects, kingdom and glory, the first the means in the offer of glory, the second the end. Kingdom is discussed in the center of the speech, glory in the outer sections.

The example of Socrates which closes the center section (3. 96–99) is Jesus' answer to the self-interested rule which Satan has proposed in the person of Alexander. Socrates' "deeds of peace" and "wisdom eminent" (3. 91) are the contrary of the heroic ideal, and his self-sacrifice contrasts with the conqueror's self-aggrandizement. The description of the destructiveness of warriors which begins the central section (3. 77–80) replies to Satan's suggestion that Jesus take Israel by force, the suggestion made through the example of Scipio. Jesus answers the broad point, the value of government by sword, rather than the narrow one, the justifiability of defensive war (*that* he later concedes). The fallacy in Satan's argument he suggests in his later reference to Scipio (3. 101–3): as Satan has praised Scipio on the basis of a single commendable aspect of his life — his deeds in isolation from the motives prompting them — so he has praised military power on the basis of a single praiseworthy kind. The example of Job, paired with that of Socrates (3. 92–95), meets Satan's call for Jesus to satisfy the "thirst of glory"; the depiction of the fate of conquerors (3. 81–87), connected with the description of their destructiveness, replies to the picture of the yet-inglorious Caesar. Jesus opposes Job's endurance to the self-indulgence Satan urges, and he describes the reality of Roman imperial life as an answer to that description of the downcast Caesar by which Satan had recommended royal luxury. Jesus also takes note of Satan's equation of pride with passional longing. When he points out that Job was "Made famous in a land and times obscure" (3. 94), he argues that glory is won not by seeking to "quench" the "thirst" for it, but by "patience" and "temperance" (3. 92).

His main refutation, though, is contained in the description of conquerors, who, he says, "swell with pride, and must be titled gods," but die "scarce men,/ Rolling in brutish vices, and deformed" (3. 81, 85–86). Though his subject is "brutish vices," passional sins, Jesus brings in the conquerors' pride to show that he sees Satan's inclusion of it among the passions. But Jesus treats pride as a delusion antithetical to the reality of emotional vice — contrasts the two evils, and thereby disposes of Satan's sophistry in equating them. He also disposes of the idea that, granting glory to be a passional end, it would be a legitimate object of desire. He ridicules the pursuers of glory, comically contrasting their superhuman pretensions with their subhuman reality, and satirically comparing them in all their pomp to bloated hogs wallowing in a sty.

The outer sections in Jesus' rejection of glory contain the poem's clearest definition of holiness. Answering Satan's reproach for "depriv[ing]" himself of "fame and glory" (3. 23–25), Jesus concludes his speech (3. 88–107) by declaring that he seeks not his own glory but God's. Citing as his example of vanity Scipio (whom Satan had validly praised as a defender of his country), Jesus turns against Satan his own praise of fame. Satan having claimed that "glory" is "the reward/ That sole excites to high attempts the flame/ Of most erected spirits" (3. 25–27), Jesus applies the claim to Scipio: "if young African for fame/ His wasted country freed from Punic rage,/ The deed becomes unpraised." Jesus' opening statement—his declaration that he seeks God's approval, not man's (3. 47–70)—answers Satan's second reproach, his claim that Jesus is "depriv[ing]/ All earth her wonder at [his] acts."

When Satan objects to the dispraise of glory, Jesus completes discussion of the subject with an explanation of how glory may be legitimately attained. The two points in his second speech relate to the two arguments in his first: that God deserves man's praise (3. 122–41) is the complement of the argument that man should seek God's praise, and that God gives glory to those who glorify him (3. 142–44) complements the argument that men should seek God's glory rather than their own. Jesus begins with God's declaration in Samuel, "them that honor me I will honor," [10] but he transforms these words into paradoxes about self-forgetfulness and self-fulfillment.

The three offers of specific kingdoms are set apart not only by the likeness in what is offered, but by a distinctive set of argumentative topics—fear, duty, and prophecy. The grouping suggests that the three offers constitute a single offer, the offer of kingdom for its own sake rather than as an end or as a means.

In his attempts to stimulate sensory self-indulgence, Satan moves from what Jesus in his definition of temperance calls "passions" to what he calls "fears." He begins this approach in the offer of Israel. Punning on the military sense of the word "retire," Satan contrasts Jesus' "retiring" with the conduct of Judas Maccabeus, who "Retired unto the desert, but with arms" (3. 163–66). Here Satan hopes to shame Jesus into an excessive denial of fear, a wrathful excess, but in the following temptations he tries the opposite tack; he proposes the indulgence of fear. In the offer of Parthia he assures Jesus that he would not arouse him "and not every way secure/ On no slight grounds [his] safety" (3. 348–49). Pointing to dangers, he recommends remedies whose acceptance would constitute an admission of fear (3. 356–70). When Jesus retorts emphatically, Satan mutes the appeal, but it appears in his opening description of the defenses of

Rome—the "citadel/ Impregnable," the "gilded battlements" of the palace (4. 47–54).

These distinctive appeals to fear are supplemented by more ordinary temptations. These, the temptations to overvalue sensory goods, are differently colored in the three offers. In presenting Israel, Satan colors matter with glory. The rise of Judas Maccabeus, "With Modin and her suburbs once content" (3. 167–70), recalls Satan's earlier references to Jesus' obscurity and to Caesar's longing for prominence. In the Roman episode, matter is colored with beauty; Satan calls attention to the craftsmanly adornments of the buildings (4. 55–60). In the offer of Parthia, Satan's pictures (3. 310–36) of "martial equipage" (3. 304) present matter in the guise of power, but there are also washes both of glory from the offer past and of luxury from the offer to come. Luxury is evoked by the honorific application of the symbol from Daniel, "golden monarchy" (3. 277),[11] by the description of the "amber stream" reserved for kings (3. 288–89), and by the enticing transferred epithet, "luxurious kings of Antioch" (3. 297).[12] Glory appears in Milton's comparison of the Parthian campaign to the besieging of Albracca in Boiardo's epic (3. 337–42). As Arnold Stein observes, Milton's comparison renders Satan's own enhancement of the scene he is presenting, and Stein's witty comparison both explains Satan's tactics and renders the sensory nature of the assault: Satan, he says, is "trying to make attractive for this second Adam a rather plain second Eve." [13]

The intellectual temptations are marked by the discussion of messianic prophecies. The basic pattern appears in the offer of Israel. Satan's request that Jesus "fulfill . . . The Prophets old" (3. 177–78) is equivalent to his first day's appeal for him to prove his identity, and the advice that Jesus "verify/ The Prophets" repeats the request for a miracle which would test God's word. (Here, though, the proposals are abstract theological arguments, rather than an old shepherd's personal pleas.) The pattern appears in three different forms in the three offers. In the offer of Israel, the plea is a religious one. In the Parthian episode, Satan equates God's prophecy with Fortune and Jesus with the hero who must urge his star. The argument is an appeal to the classical heroic tradition, though Satan tries to sanctify the pagan ideas with a biblical example, David (3. 351–56). In the offer of Rome, Satan takes the role of a practical man skeptical of idealists' dreams: "without the highest attained/ Will be for thee no sitting, or not long,/ On David's throne, be prophecied what will" (4. 105–8). Hardheaded advice and doubts replace the religious and heroic exhortations.

The distinctive elements in the rational trials, the equations of power with duty, are paired with the usual appeals to self-interested rule. These argumentative motifs also appear in variant versions. In his introduction Satan points out that Israel is now a Roman province; citing the desecration of the temple, he adds that the country has not always been governed "With temperate sway" (3. 157–63). By the first of these points Satan prepares for his later call to zeal—"Zeal of thy father's house" (3. 175): the phrase "thy father's house" refers to what Satan elsewhere calls "thy father David's house" (3. 282), not—as has been suggested [14]—to God's house (Satan mentions "father David" earlier in the speech [3. 153]). The lack of restraint and its example are picked up in Satan's call for duty, "duty to free/ Thy country from her heathen servitude" (3. 175–76). What was hinted in Satan's identification of Herod's realm—"Judah's throne/ (Thy throne)"—is made explicit in the call to zeal here, and the summons to duty makes explicit what Satan had proposed through the example of Scipio.

In presenting these pleas, Satan refers to Jesus' scorn of Alexander and of military conquest; "If kingdom move thee not," he begins (3. 171). He then offers kingdom, but applies moral, semireligious, names to self-interested and worldly power. Because Jesus does not answer directly, Satan repeats the proposal in his next offer, adding even more specificity. "Zeal of thy father's house" becomes "reinstall[ation] . . . In David's royal seat" as "his true successor" (3. 372–73); "duty to free/ Thy country" becomes the rescue of the ten lost tribes (3. 374–80). Now, however, zealotry has subsided into mere nationalism. When Jesus refuses "To rescue Israel from the Roman yoke" (1. 217), Satan, believing that he wishes "to subdue and quell o'er all the earth/ Brute violence and proud tyrannic pow'r" (1. 218–19), tenders his last and greatest realm, and broadens his appeals. For David's throne he substitutes the worldwide influence represented by the ambassadors seen converging on Rome from the ends of the earth (4. 61–89). He turns the duty to free Israel from "heathen servitude" into the duty to free Rome from "servile yoke," replaces the rescue of the ten tribes with the rescue of Rome (4. 90–104), of—as he later says—"no less than all the world" (4. 105).

When the three offers of specific kingdoms are considered as a group, they constitute the offer of kingdom for its own sake, and serve therefore as a test of the reason. In the offer of Israel the rational assault is emphasized by the dramatic nature of Jesus' reply: Jesus answers Satan's appeals to "zeal" and "duty" with what is—as Barbara Lewalski observes [15]—an unexpected direct counterattack. In the other two episodes, the rational appeals receive emphasis from the grandeur of what is refused and offered. In the Parthian offer, as A. S. P. Woodhouse notes,[16] Jesus rejects a political goal which he himself had once contemplated (1. 215–17) and which his disciples the fishermen still hold (2. 42–48). In the Roman episode Satan tenders nothing less than the chance to establish political freedom throughout the world.

But these three offers are also separate offers, differing in emphasis: Satan calls upon the intellect for reinforcement, then upon the passions, and finally he places full weight upon the reason alone. Though the differences are of course suggested in the natures of the particular countries offered, they are also indicated in the patterns of the arguments. Satan begins the offer of Israel by supplying background for his threefold temptation (3. 150–63). His statement that "powerful hands" will "not part/ Easily" with Israel introduces his reproaches to Jesus for "sitting still"; his declaration that Jesus is "to a kingdom . . . born" prepares for his exhortation that Jesus bring God's prophecy to pass; and of course the description of the Roman occupation sets up the political argument.

The introduction emphasizes not the points, however, but the relationship between them: the goal is the fulfillment of prophecy, the obstruction is Roman rule, the means of eliminating the obstruction is warfare. Stress is placed on the spiritual argument by the fact that it supplies the goal. Satan prefaces the Parthian offer with a discourse on Jesus' inexperience (3. 227–50): lack of experience, he says, explains why Jesus is so "Irresolute, unhardy, unadvent'rous." Furthermore, before Satan's argumentative speech, he describes Parthia at length (3. 267–309), concentrating on its might here as in the vision which follows; the pictures present material goods in the way relevant to Satan's concomitant appeal to fear. The introductory material gives weight to the sensory temptation. In the offer of Rome, Satan abandons the technique of reinforcement, and in this offer the sensory and spiritual attacks are submerged: a preface disposes of the former, an afterthought of the latter.

The differences between the three offers are also rendered in the metamorphoses of the arguments. In the offer of Israel, the mention of the rise of Maccabeus presents material goods in terms of glory, and the reference to the desecration of the temple places patriotism in a religious light. The spiritual cast fits the intellectual slant of the offer, and the intellectual temptation itself is treated accordingly, as a direct religious appeal. In the next trial, people and land replace the temple as the focus of the rational assault, and the intellectual argument involves not piety but heroism and destiny. The orientation fits the offer's emphasis on what Jesus calls "fleshy arm" (3. 387), and the sensory temptation itself presents material goods in terms of such military might as would reassure a cowardly messiah. In the last offer, the praise of Rome's security prepares for the demonstration of the breadth of the emperor's influence, while the beauty of the city shows the nobility of the people who require rescue from Tiberius. The sensory temptation thus prepares for the rational one, and in the picture of Tiberius, Satan meets Jesus' expected rebuttal. Describing the "Old and lascivious" emperor—his throne a "sty" (3. 90–102), Satan alludes to Jesus' description of a glory-loving conqueror in his later days, "Rolling in brutish vices, and deformed." By making Tiberius Rome's enemy, Satan links luxury with civilization rather than with brutishness, and aligns it with freedom rather than with tyranny. Satan also harmonizes his spiritual appeal with the dominant rational one. The realist skeptical of such mystical matters as prophecies ("be prophecied what will") is a Roman sophisticate, and an attractive one —as appealing in his reasonableness as the old shepherd was in his simplicity. Satan takes a pose that recommends the offered kingdom.

With regard to the offers of Israel and Parthia, Jesus weights his replies in accordance with the balances in the proposals themselves. In respect to the first, he stresses the intellectual rebuttal, and incorporates into it the answer to the less important passional attack (3. 182–97). He begins with a reply to the suggestion that he "fulfill" and "verify/ The Prophets old." Refusing to demonstrate his divinity, Jesus leaves the fulfillment of prophecies to God, and he refuses to test God, taking his declaration of faith from the "Prophet[ ] old." Daniel blessed the Lord who "changeth the times and the seasons," [17] and Jesus calls God him "in whose hand all times and seasons roll." He then turns to the sensory temptations. In reply to Satan's gibe that he shows fear by "retiring," Jesus interprets his stay in the desert as a willingly accepted "advers[ity]." His list, "tribulations, injuries [that is, calumnies], insults,/ Contempts, and scorns, and snares," though general, also refers particularly to Satan's past attempts; and Jesus ends with the tactic which Satan has yet to try, "violence." The declaration parallels Jesus' praise of "patient Job" (3. 95). Satan's reference to the rise of Maccabeus from obscurity is answered with maxims on the moral uses of lowliness: "Who best/ Can suffer best can do; best reign who first/ Well hath obeyed." This exaltation of the humble is a complement to Jesus' earlier description of conquerors, who believe that they are exalted, but end in "brutish" degradation. Jesus closes both these arguments by linking them to his original topic. By saying that adversity allows God to "know/ What [he] can suffer, how obey," he once more defines glory as God's approval of human virtue. When he says that obscurity is a "just trial ere [he] merit/ [His] exaltation without change or end" (3. 196), he again declares that God of his "bounty" (3. 142) advances man to glory. The closing arguments supplement the opening ones, forming again the paradoxes from the offer of glory: God gives glory to those who do not seek it, and those who give glory to God receive it.

The Parthian offer is opposite to the offer of Israel in its emphasis, and in replying, Jesus incorporates the intellectual rebuttal into his answer to the sensory attack (3. 387–402). He begins with references to Satan's advice on dangers ("in my ear/ [Thou hast] Vented much policy") and to Satan's display of war material ("much instrument of war . . . Before mine eyes thou hast set"). Both he rejects as ineffectual: the advice, "Plausible to the world," is specious, the armament unavailing. He then turns to Satan's religious arguments. In asserting that his "time . . . is not yet come," he repeats his earlier refusal to seize godhood, and he shows his belief in God's prophecy in the parenthetical warning to Satan: "that time for thee/ Were better farthest off." Jesus closes by bringing these religious arguments to bear on his original subject. He rejects Satan's imputation of fear, and points out that the acceptance of material power would constitute an admission of weakness—arguments for temperance which Jesus ties to his belief in God's favor and God's promise. The closing points supplement the opening ones, and as in the offer of Israel, they form paradoxes: worldly men lose the world, and unworldly men gain it. (The texts for the argument—they lie in Jeremiah [18]—are sharply antithetical, but the paradoxes are Jesus'.)

Both speeches close with forceful political replies, the explicit replies of the Parthian offer tallying with the challenging questions that end the discussion of Israel. When Jesus asks Satan why he is "solicitous" about his kingdom (3. 199–200), he suggests what he later says, that Satan is the enemy of Israel, David, and David's throne (3. 409–13). His argument is that a king ought not heed an enemy's advice; though differently expressed, the piece of political wisdom resembles Jesus' earlier statement that Satan's "gifts" are "guiles" (2. 391). In asking Satan, "Know'st thou not that my rising is thy fall" (3. 201–2), Jesus not only suggests the nature of his rule—the freeing of mankind from Satan's beguilement—but he also acts as this sort of ruler toward Satan, teaching him truths of which he is apparently ignorant. Jesus' later refusal to save the ten lost tribes (3. 414–32) is based on the same conception of kingship: Jesus' concern is the spiritual rescue which the captive tribes have refused, not the political rescue which they do not deserve.

Milton prefaces the offer of Rome with three similes (4. 10–20). Two contain in addition to their epical allusions references to old emblems. The comparison of Satan to a swarm of flies "About the wine-press" is, as Stein observes,[19] an allusion to the religious emblem for the Son as savior; the image thus treats Satan as a corrupter of intellect. The second, the comparison of Satan to waters beating against an unmovable rock, relies upon the symbolic likening of passions to a stormy sea; the image treats Satan as a sensory tempter. The main image, the most detailed, develops its allusion to Odysseus into a description of the defeat of sophistry by truth; the image bears on the main aspect of the second day's temptation, Satan's test of the reason. The desperation attributed to Satan in all three images emphasizes the fact that he is trying the last of his planned baits.

The bait is the last because Satan is thinking of the five kingdoms represented in Nebuchadnezzar's dream, the dream of a statue composed of four metals which is shattered by a stone.[20] The prophetic dream is in Satan's mind when he says that Jesus is "to a kingdom . . . born." The offer of Parthia, as Mrs. Lewalski shrewdly observes,[21] includes the offer of the first three kingdoms represented in the allegorical statue. Satan, she points out, refers to Assyria explicitly as "golden," he alludes to Persia, the second (silver) kingdom, when he mentions Cyrus and the cities of Persepolis, Bactra, and Ecbatana (3. 284–87), and when he names Selucia and Nisibus and mentions the defeated king of Antioch (3. 288–97), he refers to the Macedonian empire, the third (brazen) kingdom. Having begun with Israel, which he supposes to be the shattering stone, Satan after the rejection of Parthia has only one realm left, Rome, the fourth (iron) kingdom. When Jesus replies to the Roman offer, he shows that he recognizes Satan's plight: he argues in a way that draws the discussion of kingdoms to a close.

By giving a specific answer to Satan's central political argument, Jesus leaves no room for further exploration, and ticks off the last of the listed kingdoms. In rejecting self-interest (4. 121–25), he applies internal disproof to the specific allurement Satan has used: the ambassadors converging on Rome would only bore him with their lies, and since they are ambassadors from the ends of the earth, they would present "outlandish" lies. He refuses external rule (4. 125–45) by putting into Roman terms his warning of Satan's fall and his refusal to rescue the captive tribes: he comes not to expel an emperor but a devil, it is not his mission to rescue Rome's "inward slaves."

In answering Satan's passional attack, Jesus recapitulates the entire day's sensory temptations, as if to have done with the subject once and for all. By saying that Rome's luxury does not "allure [his] eye,/ Much less [his] mind" (4. 110–13), he notes the tactic characteristic of this particular offer, Satan's attempt to weave the sensory assault into the rational one, to turn Rome's safety and beauty into symbols of its breadth and worth. While answering the temptations proper, Jesus connects the Roman offer with the Parthian one, bracketing the gentile realms. He inserts an insinuative parenthesis into his description of a Roman banquet: "For I have also heard, perhaps have read" (4. 116). The remark comments on Satan's "concern for the timid inexperience of a rustic hero" (the words and view are Stein's): [22] Jesus is connecting the safe imperial palace in Rome with the recommendations for a Parthian alliance, and is tying both to Satan's explanation for Jesus' "irresolute, unhardy, unadven'rous" behavior. In addition, Jesus couples his rejection of Rome's luxury with a reminder of the previous guise in which Satan had offered sensory goods: "Nor doth this . . . show/ Of luxury . . . More than of arms before, allure mine eye" (4. 110–12). By suggesting, finally, what "sumptuous gluttonies" Satan could offer (4. 113–21), Jesus not only calls to mind the banquet which began the day, but also the subsequent offers of kingdom as an end and as a means. Remarking that he "hunger[s] still" (4. 121), Jesus refers to the offer of wealth, during which Satan called him "hunger-bit" (2. 416); and when he says that he "thirst[s]" (4. 120), he refers to the following offer, where Satan extolled the "thirst of glory."

Jesus' intellectual arguments draw together the references to prophecy peculiar to the offers of specific realms; Jesus thereby suggests that the discussion of nations is at an end. His closing remark, that there will be means to his kingdom—"but what the means/ Is not for thee to know, nor me to tell" (4. 152–53)—is the answer to Satan's warning that "without the highest attained" there will be "no sitting, or not long,/ On David's throne." The reply is often interpreted as Jesus' refusal to tell Satan what he knows. Elizabeth Pope argues that the lines reflect the tradition that Satan tempted Christ in order to ascertain his identity, and that Christ concealed it from him.[23] The tradition assumes that Christ is divine, while Milton portrays him, Miss Pope believes, as simply a human being.[24] But, citing Jesus' statement that "what concerns [his] knowledge God reveals" (1. 293), she argues that perhaps the means to Jesus' kingdom was a part of the revealed knowledge.[25] Mrs. Lewalski, asserting that Jesus receives intermittent illuminations from God, argues that in the lines Jesus claims "full knowledge of the means to his kingdom, which we know that he did not have as he entered the desert." [26]

It is possible, though, to view the passage as saying what Christ says in Matthew: "of [the] day and hour [of the Messiah's coming] knoweth no one, no, not the angels of heaven, but [the] Father only." [27] If the knowledge is denied to men, then only God can reveal it, and if it is denied to angels in heaven, then fallen angels cannot know it. This reading is surely preferable. It does not require the presence of un- reported events, and it is consistent with other passages in the poem — with Jesus' other refusals to exercise divinity. It is compatible with the pattern of sophistry and refutation which typifies the second day's trials, and does not entail an anomalous test of wills. Furthermore, by avoiding the child's taunt, "That's for me to know and you to find out," it saves Jesus' dignity.

In replying to Satan's warning, then, Jesus is recapitulating his previ- ous statements about means — "Means I must use, thou say'st . . . : My time, I told thee . . . is not yet come" (3. 394–97), and his earlier declaration, "If of my reign prophetic Writ hath told/ That it shall never end, so when begin/ The Father in his purpose hath decreed" (3. 184–86). In answering the other element in Satan's test, his doubt of God's word ("be prophecied what will"), Jesus quotes two prophetic texts from Daniel (4. 146–51). The act of quoting of course demon- strates Jesus' faith in God's word,[28] but through these texts Jesus also draws together both Satan's previous challenges and his own replies.

The first text concerns Nebuchadnezzar's dream of a world-over- shadowing tree.[29] The passage recalls the image of growth from Ec- clesiastes which Jesus had quoted in the Israel episode, "To every thing there is a season," [30] and it evokes the curse and blessing from Jeremiah to which he had alluded in the Parthian episode: "Cursed be the man that . . . maketh flesh his arm" but "Blessed is the man that trusteth in the Lord . . . For he shall be as a tree planted by the waters." (It is true that Jesus does not cite the end of this text, but Satan is also oblique in his allusion to Daniel: both participants know the Bible, and the reader is expected to match them in recognition.) By the image Jesus draws his own arguments to a triumphant close; and by the second passage he cites, that of the shattering stone, he refers to the prediction which Satan has been remembering, and indicates that Satan has failed to fathom it.

Satan tries his last bait, then, and Jesus not only resists but shows his awareness both of his own victory and of his opponent's failure. The conscious triumph is more than Satan can bear, and he "impudent[ly]" (4. 154) names the price for his kingdoms (4. 155–69). The display of temper matches the outburst which precedes the sequence of five offers, and marks the end of this section—the central section —of Jesus' second trial.

5

Ascension Day

DICK TAYLOR, JR., feels that critics have overemphasized both Satan's desperation and his use of violence on the third day.[1] Taylor, who believes that Satan's storm is part of a plan to cause Jesus to follow false portents,[2] also believes that afterward Satan "forcefully carr[ies] out" a further and "clever" plan. This, the trick to induce Jesus to perform an unauthorized miracle is, he says, an idea which Satan has been "holding in reserve all along."[3] Milton indicates, though, that the ominous interpretation of the storm is a spur-of-the-moment invention—Satan comes "with no new device" (4. 443)—and he also indicates that the test on the tower is not a premeditated and carefully executed stratagem: Satan acts in anger, "swoll'n with rage" (4. 499). Milton calls the storm an act of violence, an effort to "tempt the Son of God with terrors dire" (4. 431); and violence is stressed in the subsequent events. Replying to the interpretation of the storm, Jesus accuses Satan of trying to turn terrifying visions into terrifying signs (4. 486–91); and however subtle the trap on the pinnacle, it could not work without the threat of death.

But desperation and violence are not synonymous with regression here. Although Don Cameron Allen is right in noting that on the third day, Satan reneges on his resolve to use "Not force, but well-couched fraud, well-woven snares" (1. 94–97), he is wrong in concluding that Satan is a "cornered and desperate animal."[4] Satan's resolution needs to be compared with the Father's description of Jesus' coming trials;

these include "Satanic strength" as well as "All the world, and mass of sinful flesh" (1. 161–62). Satan's "snares" are the Father's lure of the "world," and when Satan has exhausted both this and the earlier lure of the "flesh," he is emotionally shattered ("swoll'n with rage") and rationally bankrupt ("with no new device"). But the "force" which Satan plans to forgo is the "Satanic strength" which the Father foresees his using. Thus on the third day Satan is not a creature without resource but a creature with one last awesome resource, the perverted will; his final state is not bestial but, as the Father says, diabolic. The fact that Satan appears undisguised on this day (4. 449) labels his state, as does the fact that Satan does not consult with his followers as he did on the preceding days: the "strength" he displays is unadulteratedly "Satanic."

From the idea of regression comes the idea that the third temptation is morally anticlimactic. Arnold Stein argues that "the terrors and the test on the tower . . . are not new temptations, and certainly not the high point in the drama of temptation." [5] But in the patristic formula the Father voices, the third temptation is the highest one, and Milton calls attention to the religious subject of the final test by attaching emblematic imagery to his descriptions of the time of day. Calling night the "Privation mere of light and absent day" (4. 400), he evokes the theological description of evil. He compares dawn to a saint who is able to overcome evil—to exorcise demons, specifically: "chas[e]" clouds, "lay" winds and phantoms (4. 426–30); and he compares the sun to God, the source of good: "now the sun with more effectual beams [than those of the dawn]/ Had cheered the face of earth" (4. 432–33).

The first day is a trial of sense, and emotional appeals typify it. The second day is a trial of the reason, and that faculty is represented not only by the kind of argument, but by the complexity of the offer, its division and subdivision: reason is the analytic faculty. The third day tries the soul's highest faculty, the intellect. The coercion which characterizes Satan's assaults represents the perverted will, intellect being the source of will. The antithesis to this coercion is fortitude. Stein says that the third day "may be considered, ethically, the test of fortitude; theologically, the general test of trust in God specialized as presumption." [6] But because fortitude demonstrates the uprightness of the will, Milton can use it as the sign of intellectual virtue, and the treatment of the day's events suggests that Milton is presenting not two tests but a single theological test. In the tower episode, Jesus' courage in refusing the consolation of a certain rescue is incorporated into his demonstration of faith, his resignation to God's will (this construction of the event will be defended later): the episode equates rather than distinguishes courage and faith. The two virtues are also equated earlier.

Milton makes walking a typifying activity of Jesus on the third day. After the storm Jesus is found "walking on a sunny hill" (4. 447), he continues walking through Satan's ominous interpretation of the storm, and he does not stop when making his own reply (4. 484–85). The activity is appropriate for this day because it integrates with the actions on the tower: "Whoso walketh uprightly shall be saved; but he that is perverse in his ways shall fall at once," says Proverbs,[7] and the image is related to the one which Satan wrenches from Psalms, the image of stumbling—"dash[ing]" one's "foot against a stone" (4. 556–59).[8] What the activity symbolizes is explained in Proverbs: "Get wisdom, get understanding. . . . Ponder the path of thy feet. . . . Turn not to the right hand nor to the left: remove thy foot from evil." [9] Walking is a metaphor for determination or persistence—a component of fortitude; but persistence is viewed in relation to wisdom, the acceptance of God's guidance. Jesus' walking thus symbolizes steadfast faith, fortitude as an aspect of holiness.[10]

Satan tests first whether the faithful man will remain temperate: his storm is primarily directed at Jesus' sensory soul. The episode thus relates to the first day's trial, and it is connected with it through the subject of the old shepherd's opening speeches, the rigors of the wilderness (1. 321–45). The two episodes are also linked by the description of Satan disguised as

> an aged man in rural weeds,
> Following, as seemed, the quest of some stray ewe,
> Or withered sticks to gather, which might serve
> Against a winter's day when winds blow keen
> To warm him wet returned from field at eve.
> (1. 314–18)

The quest of the ewe prepares for the concern of the hard-pressed shepherd for Jesus' subsistence in the barren waste; the wind and wet and need for warmth foreshadow the conditions of the storm. In addition, the storm is connected with the banquet, the second day's analogue to the opening trial. The wrath displayed during the storm is anticipated by Satan's outburst of anger after the refusal of his banquet (2. 392–403). And, as Stein has observed, banquet and storm are related by way of reversal: the storm shows nature angry, the banquet nature bountiful.[11] Details in the scenes facilitate this contrast. The delicacies of the banquet are likened to Eve's apple (2. 348–49), while later, trees which bear no fruit (pines and oaks) are uprooted by a storm evocative of the opposite end of time, the world's last day: "water with fire/ In ruin reconciled" (4. 409–21). Satan's splendid banquet was "no dream" (2. 337), while later Satan presents a dreamed ugliness (4. 407–9). Jesus, served earlier by attentive and seductive deities (2. 350–61), is now besieged by hellish shapes, hostile or repulsive (4. 421–25).

The sensory soul, appropriately, receives the brunt of the night's attacks, though as always Satan tries all Jesus' faculties. The diabolic "specters" (4. 430) attack the intellect—the menacing furies encouraging self-concern, the howling ghosts a distrust of God's favor or his power; they tempt Jesus to defend himself with a self-directed and distrustful miracle. The "ugly dreams" present distorted ideas to Jesus' reason in its unwatchful state. The lightning, wind, and rain attack the sense. These natural "terror[s]" inspire fear, of course, and they also encourage an excessive longing for warmth and shelter, the physical need which ranks with food as a necessity of life; Milton draws attention to this element of the temptation when he comments, "Ill was thou shrouded [sheltered] then, O patient Son of God." Since the dreams and phantoms are devices for increasing the storm's effectiveness, the storm itself provides the main assault.

After the storm Satan appears and interprets it (4. 451–83). His interpretation relies on arguments from the face-saving prediction, Satan's epilogue to the second day's trial. The first part of that prediction (4. 374–81) is a reproach to Jesus for rejecting offered good. It mingles three claims: Jesus should avoid pain and exertion, he should accept Satan's aid and receive Israel or the world, he must seize the proper hour and honor God's prophecies. The second section (4. 382–93) is a warning on the bad effects of the rejection. The same arguments are repeated negatively: Jesus will reap pain and toil; he will never obtain the promised kingdom—a kingdom of doubtful reality anyway; he has lost his time, and heaven promises only evil for him. In his interpretation of the storm Satan repeats the negative series. His sensory attack is the prediction of laborious distress ("hard assay/ Of dangers") and of distressing labor ("adversities and pains") (4. 477–80). The warnings of suffering are an appeal to fear, the warnings of labor an incitement to material comfort. The political assault is Satan's sarcastic prediction of success: "Thou shalt be what thou art ordained, no doubt;/ For angels have proclaimed it, but concealing/ The time and means" (4. 472–75).[12] The statement echoes Satan's earlier sarcasm:

> A kingdom they [the stars] portend thee, but what kingdom,
> Real or allegoric, I discern not,
> Nor when; eternal sure, as without end,
> Without beginning; for no date prefixed
> Directs me in the starry rubric set.
>
> (4. 389–93)

In the present gibe, Satan implies that if Jesus does not take the means at hand he will never attain power; Satan also suggests that the sort of rule predicted by angels is not rule in this world. Satan's religious attack is his claim that Jesus is bent on gaining his kingdom "no man knows when" and is "prolong[ing] all to the push of fate" (4. 469–72): Jesus does not know God's intent, he will act not at God's time but when forced by circumstance.

There is, of course, nothing new in Satan's arguments. They are avowedly a repetition: "Did I not tell thee," "be sure to find/ What I foretold thee" (4. 468, 477–78); and even in their earlier appearance they were a précis of already-rejected appeals. What *is* new is the element of coercion provided by the storm. In his introductory discussion of the event Satan underlays his coming arguments. In order to incite fear and love of ease, Satan calls attention to Jesus' physical discomfort with a spiteful innuendo: storms, he says, are as "harmless . . . as a sneeze/ To man's less universe" (4. 454–59). When he claims to have been absent during the night of dangers (4. 451–54), Satan encourages Jesus to worry that, having rejected a willing helper, he has become the powerless possessor of empty promises. Discussing the ominousness of storms (4. 460–66), he suggests that Jesus has betrayed God and received God's curse. At the end of the speech, Satan returns to the "terrors, voices, prodigies" of the night (4. 481–83). By "terrors" he designates the natural disorders; these, he implies, tell of physical hardships to come. The "voices" are the dreams which he had whispered in Jesus' ear; they warn of impotence and false expectation. In "prodigies" Satan refers to the fiendish shapes, tokens of divine rejection. Closing as he opened, Satan surrounds his arguments with threats.

By this coercion Satan pits his will against all Jesus' faculties, but his primary target is the reason. His thesis is a piece of practical advice:

"Each act is rightliest done,/ Not when it must, but when it may be best" (4. 475–76); means are at hand, the realm can be won, and therefore Jesus should act. Satan's aim is to push Jesus into reconsidering his rejection of the world's kingdoms. In subject, therefore, this speech recalls the second day's trial, and the analogy is made obvious by the relation of the warning to Satan's face-saving prediction, the résumé of the second day's arguments.

As the storm is a wordless temptation, Jesus' reaction is a wordless reply. The hellish visions do not provoke a rash and distrustful miracle; Jesus sits in "calm and sinless peace" (4. 424–25). The force of the storm does not break Jesus' self-control: though the pines and oaks "Bow[ ] their stiff necks," Jesus "st[an]d[s]/ Unshaken," and though "Ill . . . shrouded," he is "patient" (4. 416–21). As to the ugly dreams, the fact that Satan starts with these suggests that his aim is to increase Jesus' susceptibility to the terrifying storm to come. Although Jesus' response is not explicitly noted, his later lack of fear proves that the tactic fails. Jesus makes a verbal reply as well as this mute one, though, for he answers the references to the storm with which Satan backs his ominous predictions. "Me worse than wet thou find'st not," he begins (4. 486), dismissing the sensory trial particularly, but by implication the other trials as well. Only the material events left a mark, he implies, and that mark was only a physical one: his emotions were untouched.

Afterward he is explicit about the dreams and visions. "[Thou] storm'st," he says (4. 496), answering Satan's lie that he was "distant" from the "wrack" (4. 452–54). He views Satan not as an absent friend but as a harassing enemy, and he brings to light Satan's aim, to "terrify" him "to [his] will" (4. 496–97). When Jesus says that the phantoms, "threat'ning nigh" and "noising loud," did no "harm" (4. 486–89), he shows that he perceives Satan's intention to panic him into an unwarranted defense. Stripped of the threats, the arguments of Satan's speech are old and feeble, and Jesus disposes of them quickly: the supposed signs of divine disfavor and rejection are fraudulent (4. 489–91); Satan's aid is a snare and Satan himself knows that Jesus' reign is real (4. 492–99); and Jesus is no worse than wet—he has not caught his death of cold, he is not shivering at the future.

The climactic episode of the third temptation, the tower scene, is Satan's principal test of the intellect. Both the trial and Jesus' response have been debated—the trial in regard to the issue raised by it and in regard to Satan's tactics. There are disputes as to whether Satan's assault tests Jesus' identity or is a moral trial, and disputes as to whether Satan works simply or lays a trap.

As Elizabeth Pope shows, the traditional theological view of the test is that the devil made a straightforward moral trial of Christ: he urged him to throw himself into danger from a safe station, in order to prove that angels would rescue him.[13] John Carey argues that the episode in *Paradise Regained* presents this kind of simple moral test. He suggests that Milton may have been thinking of Josephus' account of the dizzying view from a royal portico near the temple at Jerusalem, rather than of his description of the temple's sharpened spires (this last, Miss Pope's explanation,[14] is the usual one). Carey concedes that the pinnacle described is "too small for a man to stand firmly," and he notes that Satan stands "to see" Jesus "fall" (4. 571). But, citing Jesus' rescue by the angels, who "received him soft/ From his uneasy station" (4. 582–85), Carey argues that the words "uneasy station" imply that Jesus has been standing by a "balancing feat."[15] This theory is implausible. Satan not only expects to see Jesus fall, he is so "smitten with amazement" that he topples off the roof (4. 562)—an excessive response to anything less than an impossibility. "[U]neasy station" describes the spire itself, not Jesus' feelings: the station is "uneasy" not because Jesus is wobbling uncomfortably but because a man cannot stand there.

The view that the episode is a straightforward test of identity is much more plausible. This view is succinctly stated by Allen, who says that when Satan sets Jesus upon the spire, "it is poorly concealed murder and nothing else that he has in mind":[16] Satan will prove Jesus mortal by killing him. The problem with the interpretation lies in its account of Satan's counterproposal. Developing Gilbert's interpretation, Miss Pope argues that Satan's "There stand" (4. 551) is "mere sarcasm, intended to show the real nature of what follows: 'If not to stand, cast thyself down' [4. 554–55]."[17] This reading does not account for the elaboration of the invitation to stand, an elaboration which sarcasm alone cannot explain: "I to thy [f]ather's house/ Have brought thee" (4. 452–54).[18]

The third view is more inclusive, the view that in testing Jesus' identity, Satan lays a trap. Satan believes—so Barbara Lewalski explains—that "he has allowed for all the possibilities": if Jesus is merely human he will fall, if he is divine he will perform a miracle, and "if he is uncertain he may cast himself down to test himself and God."[19] But though this is the more satisfactory of the two formulations of the identity test, that theory is open to thematic and structural objections. An extended moral debate is the most prominent element in *Paradise Regained,* and this fact suggests that the poem has an ethical aim. If the tower episode is simply a test of whether Jesus is mortal or divine, it has no ethical point. Thus it follows from the identity theory that *Paradise Regained* abandons its aim at a structurally crucial point, the climactic episode of the highest test. Furthermore, the evidence that the scene *is* only a test of identity is not compelling.

Proponents frequently begin—as Miss Pope does [20]—with Satan's own statement of his aim: "Therefore to know what more thou art than man . . . Another method I must now begin" (4. 538–40). But first of all, though what Satan says is true—he *is* interested in Jesus' identity [21]—what he says is not the whole truth. Satan is introducing the second alternative of his temptation speech, and though this alternative does involve an assertion of identity, it is also a moral snare. In the second place, God rather than Satan is the character whose intentions reveal the meaning of the scene, and God's intention is that Jesus should "o'ercome Satanic strength" (1. 161) and prove by his moral perfection that he is "by merit called [the] Son [of God]" (1. 163–66); the statement points to a moral demonstration, not to a factual one. There is in fact an ironic contrast between what Satan intends and what he accomplishes. Intending to force Jesus into a declaration of divinity, Satan provides an example of "Satanic strength" for Jesus to overcome —overcome not by a show of divinity but by a manifestation of perfect human virtue. Intending to cause Jesus to reveal "what more . . . than man" he is, he proves that Jesus is the Son of God not in power or in consciousness but "by merit."

The fourth view of the episode, that Satan's assault is both a trap and a trial, is the most satisfactory view. Miss Pope argues that Milton's use of the spire makes an ethical reading of the scene impossible: Jesus cannot reply "I will not tempt God" if he cannot help falling.[22] This argument is not subtle enough morally. As both Taylor and Stein note, what counts in a forced fall is the state of mind of the victim.[23] Jesus can remain innocent if he leaves the outcome to God; if he presumptuously thinks that God must act to save him, he yields to Satan's temptation. The trap, as Taylor sees it, is that Jesus must either perform an impious miracle or in falling make an impious appeal for divine aid.[24] Stein, agreeing, adds that Jesus may choose to stand by human means, but then will be forced to decide between the evil alternatives.[25]

Neither of these accounts relates the trial to the poem's tripartite patterning, however, and when the trap is examined in this light, it proves to be even more complex. Satan begins, as Gilbert observed,[26] with a sarcastic taunt: "There stand, if thou wilt stand; to stand upright/ Will ask thee skill" (4. 551–52). "To stand upright" puns on the moral meanings of the words, and alludes to Jesus' praise of temperate self-rule (2. 466–67): the statement contains Satan's sensory attack. The point of the taunt is that in falling, Jesus will be frightened and will reach for the spire; his fear will violate virtuous self-control, and his attempt to hold the spire will constitute a clinging to material things, for not only will the gesture show a reluctance to leave the sensory life, but under the circumstances the spire itself will become a symbol of wealth: it is a spire of gold (4. 548). The second section presents Satan's first alternative, that Jesus should stand miraculously. "Highest is best" (4. 553) is a political maxim, and the context therefore suggests that when Satan says he has brought Jesus to his "[f]ather's house," he is referring not to God's dwelling but to the house which Solomon built ("Solomon built [God] an house").[27] The placement is a symbolic coronation: Jesus, the "son of David, virgin-born" (4. 500), is brought to the house of the son of David, and "highest placed" (4. 553). This horn of the dilemma presents Satan's rational attack: if Jesus stands, he will claim the throne of David ("thy throne" [2. 425]), and claim it in order that he may benefit himself; he will also accept the sort of power which "highest is best" commends. But "show thy progeny" (4. 554) is a trap. Satan has set up alternative views of Jesus' "progeny": "hear, O son of David . . . For Son of God to me is yet in doubt" (4. 500–501). If Jesus asserts that he is the son of David, he must do so by a supernatural act which would prove him the Son of God; thus his assertion would be a lie. Satan closes his speech (4. 554–59) with his second alternative, that Jesus fall. This horn plainly presents Satan's intellectual attack. Jesus is asked to prove his identity ("safely if Son of God") and to test God's word ("For it is written"). This alternative is a trap as well. If Jesus claims divinity by falling in confidence of rescue, then he is betraying God; his claim of godliness would prove him mortal, and it would bring his mortal end.

The test on the pinnacle, Satan's primary test of intellect, is linked to the episodes which prefigure it. In the transition to the offer of learning, Satan referred to the ambiguous meaning of the term "Son of God" (4. 196–205), and he returns to that ambiguity before the tower scene. In closing the first day (1. 468–92), Satan laid a trap, and here he repeats the tactic.[28] The tower scene is made central by the fact that it epitomizes "Satanic strength." Strength can do no more than kill, and at this point alone is death immediately threatened. The trap which Satan sets, furthermore, is much more intricate than the one with which he ended the first day. There he opposed two evil alternatives, but here each alternative is itself a trap. There the sensory temptation, the least important element, did not tighten the snare, but here even this element contributes: if Jesus falls, he must either fall sure or unsure of rescue, and if he falls sure he tempts God, and if he falls unsure he displays intemperance. So intricate is the trap that "fiendish" is the natural word to apply to it, and that, of course, is the structurally apposite word.

Jesus' reply is as problematic as the test; both words and deeds have been debated. Jesus' suspension on the spire is clearly miraculous (Carey's contrary theory is untenable), but critics have disagreed as to the nature of the miracle, some claiming that Jesus performs it, some that it is a joint act of God and Jesus, some that the miracle is God's alone. They have also disagreed over the meaning of Jesus' "Tempt not the Lord thy God" (4. 561), some arguing that Jesus refers to himself, some that he refers both to himself and to God, some that he refers to God alone.

The idea that Jesus stands by miracle and proclaims himself Lord involves a misapprehension of the structure of *Paradise Regained.* A. S. P. Woodhouse says that the miracle provides a "long-awaited demonstration of divinity," [29] and Miss Pope claims that for the miracle to be "accompanied by an unequivocal announcement of Christ's divinity" is "highly dramatic." [30] God's words early in *Paradise Regained* provide a synopsis of the poem: "weakness" is to overcome flesh, world, and "Satanic strength" (1. 161–62). This outline should prevent the reader from awaiting a climax in which the hero throws off the mask of "weakness," defeats the villain with a display of powerful magic, and announces that he is really the Omnipotent in disguise.

When Satan first requests a miracle, Jesus replies, "Why dost thou . . . suggest to me distrust,/ Knowing who I am, as I know who thou art?" (1. 354–55). That a demonstration of divinity is vanity and distrust is repeated thereafter: the doctrine constitutes a strong thematic objection to the theory that Jesus announces and proves his godhood. Proponents of the theory offer no convincing counterargument. Claiming that Satan's injunction to stand is ironic, Woodhouse asserts that Jesus replies ironically, "comply[ing] with Satan's suggestion . . . not in surrender to Satan" but "in obedience to God." [31] This argument oversimplifies Satan's speech. "There stand" *is* sarcastic, but it is not an invitation to miracle. "[S]how thy progeny" invites a miracle, but it is not sarcastic; if Jesus complies, he makes the self-contradictory assertion which Satan proposes, the miraculous demonstration that he is the son of David.

Miss Pope argues that because Satan violates the rules of temptation, Jesus is freed from the necessity of responding quasi homo; the
episode, she says, "has no exemplary function." [32] If it were true that
the reading allowed the tower scene no moral significance, that fact
would be a serious drawback to the theory. It is not true, however, and
therein lies a different objection. Satan's threat of death poses a moral
problem: what is one to do if faced with the choice of death or sinning?
When Miss Pope argues that Satan's rule-breaking excuses Jesus', she
provides the episode with an exemplary function. Its moral (alas) is:
in life-and-death matters, cheat.

A final objection to this reading is the lack of corroborating evidence. The theory entails a change of rules: Jesus may now say and
do things previously forbidden him (Woodhouse claims that at this
point Jesus is given a special exemption, like the permission given
Samson to attend Dagon's rite).[33] The reader, however, must be informed of so drastic a change: if there is no explicit discussion, like
that in *Samson Agonistes*,[34] confirmation must be provided in the subsequent events. If Jesus can call himself God and perform feats of levita-
tion, then he should summon the angels, announce his supremacy on
earth, and share a table of miraculous food, turning the fallen oak trees
into steaks. The absence of such boasts and wonders is proof—as
Taylor has observed [35]—that Jesus is bound in the end by the same
rules which bound him earlier.

There are two versions of the theory that Jesus' standing is a mixed
act and his words double in their reference. The less satisfactory views
the incident in terms of Jesus' progressive illumination. Describing
Jesus as "sustained . . . by the Father" and as "exercis[ing] [his] divine
power in standing," Mrs. Lewalski claims that at the time of the miracle
the Father gives Jesus the last in a series of revelations about his
Sonship. This account of the event correlates with Mrs. Lewalski's view
of the speech; Jesus, she says, both refers to the Father, replying to
Satan's temptation to presumption, and refers to himself, announcing
his divinity.[36] In handling the dilemma which Satan sets, Mrs. Lewalski
is less adroit than Woodhouse. She argues that Jesus does not obey
Satan because he does not choose "a miraculous escape on Satan's
terms" but instead "maintain[s] the impossible position into which
Satan has thrust him." [37] Though she interprets "show thy progeny"
as an invitation to miracle,[38] Mrs. Lewalski apparently glosses the
phrase as an invitation not to a miraculous stand but to a miraculous
descent. This construction is strained, given the subsequent alternatives: "if not to stand,/ Cast thyself down" (4. 554–55). A more impor-

tant flaw is the fact that Jesus' words as Mrs. Lewalski interprets them contain a moral confusion rather than a pregnant ambiguity. If Jesus proclaims his divinity and displays it in a miracle while at the same time answering "Satan's temptation to presumptuous action," [39] he declares that it is presumption to expect a miraculous escape, but not presumption to perform it. (The theory that Jesus receives divine illuminations is itself dubious, but that question requires a separate examination.)

More satisfactory is the version of the theory which views the incident as a sudden epiphany. Avoiding the usual moral pitfalls, Stein argues that Jesus' words have two meanings, and that these are sequential: Jesus tells Satan not to tempt the Father, then is transformed into the untemptable Lord. Viewing the miracle as a sudden transfiguration of Jesus, Stein emphasizes that the "epiphany" occurs "not as an act of will, not from the self." [40] It may be objected that in this account, an event without exemplary meaning — the unique miracle — steals attention from the exemplary moral victory; but the main objection to the proposal is the lack of corroborative evidence. An unexpected and momentous change in Jesus' nature — Stein calls the event "surprising" [41] — must be made clear to the reader, and again the subsequent incidents are the place to look for confirmation. Not only do the comforts of the banquet scene relate to Jesus' human trials — the banquet (*pace* Steadman) [42] tends his human weariness and hunger (4. 591–92) — but even the angels who uphold Jesus (4. 581–85) only fulfill a promise made to any faithful man, the promise Satan has invoked from Psalms.

The most satisfactory explanation of Jesus' suspension on the tower is that one provided by Taylor: that after Jesus' moral decision, God "enters with his grace . . . and performs himself the miracle that holds Christ standing aloft on the impossible foothold of the pinnacle." [43] This reading can be justified on structural grounds. The event has been prepared for by Jesus' pronouncement on glory: "so much bounty is in God, such grace,/ That who advance his glory, not their own,/ Them he himself to glory will advance" (3. 142–44). It has also been prepared for by the symmetrical incidents in the introduction and conclusion of the poem. As Satan's opening council (1. 33–118) is balanced by his final return (4. 577–80), and the angels' first hymn (1. 168–82) by their second (4. 593–635), so God's appearance at the opening (1. 126–67) is balanced by his closing appearance — his descent to perform the miracle. The interpretation is also thematically appropriate. God's miracle provides a conclusive affirmation of the values which Jesus has exemplified. Because this trial is the supreme intellectual test, the central point is the affirmation of Jesus' pronouncement on glory. But because the test is a triple one, the miracle proves not only that God will "deliver" and "honor" the man who "hath set his love upon [him]," [44] but other truths as well. Since Satan has turned Jesus' station into a symbolic enthronement, Jesus in standing not by his own power but by God's grace proves that "those who wait upon the Lord shall inherit the earth." [45] And since Satan has tested Jesus' temperance with physical threats, God's miracle proves that the man who is "not . . . afraid what man can do unto [him]" can trust God to "deliver [his] feet from falling, that [he] may walk before God in the light of the living." [46] Grace here manifests God's will that material things go to the temperate, rule to the just, and glory to the holy.

Finally, it is possible to understand why Milton chose not to describe or even to mention God's descent, but instead narrated the incident in the way that he narrates the scene of Satan's arrival in the desert (1. 314–20), describing only what meets the eye. God's untrumpeted appearance allows the focus to remain on Jesus, whose moral victory is more important than the divine judgment which validates it. The high point of the poem, both from a thematic and from a structural standpoint, is not Jesus' rescue, but Jesus' manifestation of perfect temperance, justice, and holiness.

The most satisfactory reading of the phrase "Tempt not the Lord" is this view that it refers only to God the Father. Jesus answers Satan's challenge, Taylor explains, by "leav[ing] the outcome of [the] event to God"; he performs neither the act of miraculously standing nor the act of voluntarily falling, and tells Satan not to tempt the Father.[47] Jesus perceives that "Satan is really striking at God and at God's order through himself," Taylor claims,[48] construing Jesus' quotation as an imperative directed at Satan. An alternative reading is possible, though. Conventionally—so Miss Pope observes—Christ's words are taken to mean "I refuse to make a trial of God." [49] Miss Pope asserts that if Jesus cannot help fall, this answer is meaningless,[50] but Jesus may meaningfully refuse the willingness to fall as distinguished from the act of falling. The phrase as Taylor reads it, with its command and its implicit appeal for aid, does not provide a convincing illustration of that perfect resignation which Taylor rightly ascribes to Jesus. A more powerful illustration results from the conventional reading: Jesus thinks not of his own status but of God's will, and he shows his faith by a final citation of God's words.

When Jesus' response is looked at in terms of the tripartite temptation, it is even more impressive. By not accepting Satan's invitation
to fall in confidence, Jesus refuses to display his glorious status or to
test God's words; by refusing to perform a miracle, he does not seek
rule self-interestedly or pursue worldly power; and by neither flinching
nor reaching out, he shows a temperate control of fear and a temperate
mastery of sensory longings. Thus he avoids all Satan's traps: he accepts neither the alternative of falling willingly nor that of standing
by miracle, and though not falling willingly he nevertheless refuses to
fear falling; by refusing to assert his divinity, he does not show a human
frailty, nor does he perform the contradictory act of asserting temporal
rule by a supernatural feat. He avoids these snares, furthermore, not
by verbal trickery or by power—the signs of Satan's perverted will—
but by simple moral rectitude in the most extreme of circumstances.
Jesus acts temperately, unambitiously, and faithfully when it seems that
life lies in intemperance or ambition or in pride: he overcomes by
"weakness" Satan's might. This awesome and moving example of human virtue provides a thematically and structurally appropriate end
to the three days' test: it provides the poem not only with a *moral*
climax, but with a moral *climax*.

Wings

THE MINOR characters of *Paradise Regained* may be explained in terms of their bearing on the poem's schematic structure. God clarifies the patterning as a whole: his final entry marks the completion of the three-part sequence announced in his opening speech (1. 161–62). The other characters illuminate separate sections of the pattern. The entrance of the angels to carry Jesus from the tower (4. 581–85) clarifies the third trial, emphasizing the poem's climactic example of virtue. Belial's recommendation to the demonian council (2. 153–71) generalizes the trial of the flesh and helps to divide it from the offer of the world, thereby clarifying the first temptation. Mary and the disciples provide a complex introduction to the most complex temptation.

The figures in the first of the inductions to the second day (2. 1–114) form a scale of ignorance about Jesus' role as savior. The fishermen, first in the series, show the greatest ignorance; they view the messiah's mission as the military rescue of Israel (2. 42–48). Mary has a greater understanding of Jesus' rule. It is true that her meditation is permeated by political literalism. She views the stable at Bethlehem as an incongruous shelter for a king and a queen-mother, she sees the flight into Egypt as the product of dynastic rivalry, and she says of Jesus' retired life that it has been "Little suspicious to any king" (2. 82–91). The fact that she contrasts the foretold "trouble" with a change "To honor" shows that she interprets literally Simon's announcement of "the fall and rising . . . of many in Israel"; and when she refers to the "sword" which shall pierce "through [her] very soul," she expects — so her phraseology suggests — not simply overwhelming grief, but a violent end as well.

This literal conception of Jesus' rule coincides with Mary's literal-minded reaction to her son's statement that he "went about/ His Father's business" (2. 96–100). Supposing that he referred to Joseph's business, she wondered "what he meant." What raises Mary above the disciples is her sense that this literal understanding is inadequate. In her awareness of the paradoxes of her rank — that her "honor high" is an advance to "sorrow," that her "favored lot" is an "exaltation to afflictions high" (2. 66–74, 91–94) — Mary sees her difference from worldly queens; and in reinterpreting Jesus' words, she dimly perceives his "more heavenly" idea of rule (1. 221–23).

Of Jesus' higher role of savior, however, Mary is almost completely ignorant. That there *is* a higher role she guesses. She supposes that Jesus has some purpose in mind greater than the purpose for his earlier absence (2. 101–2), and in this she is correct: Jesus' purpose is to meditate his "godlike office" (1. 183–95). But Mary does not know what this role is. Her mundane interpretation of Gabriel's words and of the Father's acknowledgment of his Son (2. 66–74, 82–86) is contrasted with Jesus' spiritual readings (1. 229–89).

Jesus, the final figure in the series, is the least ignorant. Knowing that his "end of being on earth" is not to bring political freedom and not merely to bring enlightenment, he nevertheless does not know "How to begin" his "mission high" (2. 109–14). This scale relates to the coming trial. When Satan presents the kingdoms of the world, he believes what the fishermen believe of Jesus' rule. Jesus' replies are a clear formulation of what Mary dimly sees about his reign, but only at the end does Satan comprehend this view. Satan returns again and again to the prophecies of Jesus' higher mission, but except at one dramatic moment he understands no more than Mary does; Jesus' comprehension, though limited, far exceeds his tempter's.

But if the minor characters have schematic uses, they also have dramatic functions. Belial's appetitive excess casts light on Satan's condition after his first trial of Jesus, and Belial not only serves to generalize the first temptation but proves dramatically that Jesus is as impervious to masculine lust as he is to feminine gluttony. No one can imagine the self-controlled Jesus extolling women as Belial does:

> Many are in each region passing fair
> As the noon sky, more like to goddesses

Than mortal creatures, graceful and discreet,
Expert in amorous arts, enchanting tongues
Persuasive, virgin majesty with mild
And sweet allayed.

(2. 155–60)

The disciples and Mary are the natural subjects for Jesus' realm. Their resignation to God's will (2. 49–57, 94) proves that they have what Jesus calls "willing hearts" (1. 221–22), but their ignorance reveals their need for his instruction. At one important point the ignorance of these saved sets off the knowledge of the damned. But their broader function is, as Arnold Stein observes, to show what is at stake for mankind in the second temptation, "what [Jesus'] victory or defeat will mean for the waiting world of men." [1] Milton points up this dramatic function; he ends the speeches of Mary and the disciples with their desire for Jesus' restoration (2. 57, 102), and he ends the poem with the return of Jesus "Home to his mother's house" (4. 639) — a return which installs and castles the ruler. God and the angels have more vital, though less subtle, roles: God provides the story with a *deus ex machina* ending, and the angels are the vehicles whereby Jesus is rewarded for his victory. In addition, the angels serve to suggest the reality of Jesus' struggles. In the opening hymn they view Jesus as a fellow creature who, "untried," must face terrible dangers, "whate'er may tempt, whate'er seduce,/ Allure, or terrify, or undermine" (1. 176–79); though they do not doubt the Father's confidence, they nevertheless pray for Jesus' success (1. 180–81).

Viewed in one way, the central characters of *Paradise Regained* are merely vehicles for the moral arguments they voice, arguments which are significant in themselves and which are, in fact, the most prominent element in the poem. Ultimately, however, *Paradise Regained* is not a *débat* but an epic; it does have characters and an action. The structure of this narrative is no less problematic than the poem's schematic structure, however, and the first question which needs answering is what the poem's action is. Some critics, subordinating Jesus' trials to their supposed effects upon him, view the action as the protagonist's growth to knowledge. Some hold that the action is simply the proving of Jesus.

There are great aesthetic advantages to the theory that Jesus develops — not the least of these the symmetrical opposition of protagonist and antagonist: Jesus waxes as Satan wanes. Two versions of the theory have been offered, but neither, unfortunately, will bear close scrutiny.

Don Cameron Allen and Barbara Lewalski combine the developmental theory with the theory that Jesus has a unique dual nature; they argue that Jesus' divine nature is gradually restored to him by divine revelation. This interpretation has undesirable thematic consequences.

Mrs. Lewalski says that "Christ's action of overcoming the Satanic temptations in the wilderness is inextricably linked with his emerging understanding of his nature and mission." [2] The phrasing suggests that the writer is thinking of the *bildungsroman,* but the evocation is deceptive. Since in this reading Jesus has a unique nature and discovers that nature by a unique process, his growth and self-discovery have no exemplary significance; they have nothing to do with ordinary human maturation. If *Paradise Regained* has this sort of action, it can only be a historical re-creation or an ecclesiastical allegory. Viewing the poem as Milton's "illustrat[ion] [of] the unillustratable," the "mysteries" of incarnation and hypostasis,[3] Allen takes the historical view. Although Mrs. Lewalski insists that "the 'identity motif' is not a minor theme . . . but is the very substance of the dramatic action," [4] she derives the poem's meaning not from Jesus' self-discovery but from his symbolic significance; she adopts the allegorical reading proposed by Howard Schultz. These approaches not only misrepresent the work, but seriously attenuate its meaning.[5]

Stein, who holds that Jesus is a human being, summarizes his development thus: "Christ holds heroically to his wisdom, and advances from intuition to confirmation, passing through the dangerous trial of translating intuition into what will be the greatest public good, and doing so without any merely human substitutions or additions, whether the prompting comes from his own early hopes for heroic acts, or whether from the external suggestions of Satan." [6] In this version of the developmental theory, Jesus' life does have an exemplary significance.

Nevertheless, Stein's particular interpretation of the life can be questioned. His first major piece of evidence is the retrospective portion of Jesus' first soliloquy (1. 201–89), which Stein interprets as distinguishing four stages of knowledge. The first stage is the child's instinctive desire to "learn-know-do," the next—the study of the Law—a "discursive and disciplined" verification of this intuition. The third stage, the yearning for heroic deeds, is an application of the initial desire to specific ends; "unconvincing" as intuition, this stage is a "human substitution" for the first one. The last stage, the "redefin[ition]" of the "public good in terms of knowledge," is a return to the first stage, but with "the support of a fuller human discipline of reason and intellectual experience." The revelations of Mary and the subsequent study of the Bible do not, Stein says, constitute a further stage.[7]

The main objection to this reading is that it does not honor the structure of the speech. The first section in the recollection contrasts the "play" expected of the child with Jesus' own seriousness (1. 201–6). The evidences of the seriousness serve as an index to the coming section: Jesus' eagerness "to learn and know" foreshadows his study of the Law, the desire to "do/ What might be public good" anticipates his desire to free Israel and the world, and Jesus' sense that he was "born to promote all truth" introduces his idea of "teach[ing] the erring soul." The second section, then, shows the boyhood development of the child's three desires (1. 206–26). A third section begins with Mary's revelation. That it constitutes a new stage of growth is suggested by the fact that Jesus reports new insights:

> This having heard, straight I again revolved
> The Law and Prophets, searching what was writ
> Concerning the Messiah, to our scribes
> Known partly, and soon found of whom they spake
> I am.
>
> (1. 259–63)

The recollection contains three sections, then, not four, its final section comprising the portion of the speech which Stein disregards.

Stein's second major piece of evidence is the second temptation. Refining and elaborating the view of Northrop Frye, who says that by refusing Satan's offers, Jesus achieves a "negative clarification of [his] thoughts," [8] Stein argues that throughout the trial Jesus "teach[es] himself as a preparation for his end of teaching in the world," and he claims that Jesus' "concept of persuasion . . . deepen[s]," that he learns that he "is to teach without temporal office, and not the law but the inspired word, the wondrous call." [9] This reading exaggerates the extent of Jesus' change. Satan, myopically concerned with power (as Stein himself observes),[10] proffers the same sort of rule throughout the heart of the second temptation. The issue he raises, the question of spiritual and carnal rule, is one which Jesus had long ago considered; he had decided on the "humane" and "heavenly" course of "conquer[ing] willing hearts" by "winning words" (1. 221–22). Jesus does not learn—does not shift position under the pressure of new arguments; he refuses to be misled—rejects the varying exemplifications of a single false position. Trial is illustrated, not growth.

If Jesus is conceived of as a human being, the theory that he grows provides a meaningful interpretation of the poem. There are, however, strong objections not only to Stein's particular version of the theory, but to the theory itself. The first objection stems from the degree of perfection attributed to Jesus before his temptation in the wilderness. Even Stein says of Jesus' first soliloquy that "Christ, in his own developing progress toward knowledge, though the reasoning has not been tested by action, has already passed beyond the range of what will be offered." [11] Jesus is portrayed not as a man in need of wisdom, but as a man of wisdom ready for trial. The second objection lies in the poem's explicit announcements of its subject. The argument proclaims that the action of *Paradise Regained* is "one man's firm obedience fully tried/ Through all temptation" (1. 4–5), and God, the one character whose interpretation of events cannot be doubted, states that Jesus is to "o'ercome Satanic strength/ And all the world, and mass of sinful flesh" (1. 161–62). Moral trial is announced, rather than growth of knowledge.

These announcements are so explicit, in fact, that the action would never have been disputed had it not been for Merritt Hughes's construction of the poem's values: *"Contemptus mundi* was never carried further by medieval pope or doctor of the church than it was by Milton in this poem." [12] This view—it has recently been reasserted by John Steadman [13]—lies behind Stein's insistence that *Paradise Regained* deals with "heroic knowledge," not "heroic rejection," [14] and it lies behind Schultz's even more drastic conclusion that *Paradise Regained* is an allegory. Interpreted literally, he says, it teaches "without reservation" that "money, fame, political power and prestige are none of Christ's." [15] Even if Hughes's contention were true, Milton's statement of theme and God's synopsis would be evidence too strong for circumvention; but Hughes's contention is not valid, and with it goes the main objection to the theory that the poem's action is Jesus' trial.

Passional virtue is defined by Jesus' pronouncement that it is kingly to "rule[ ]/ Passions, desires, and fears" (2. 466–67). The metaphor preaches the regulation of the emotions, not the ascetic annihilation of them. In defining rational virtue, Jesus praises worldly rulers when they bear the burdens of office for the public good (2. 457–65), and when he rejects political office, he rejects it not for thoughts of the next world but for an alternative form of service in this world, the work of moral instruction (2. 473–80). Jesus' praise of the refusers of kingdom (2. 481–83) is not a rejection of secular service. In his praise Jesus alludes to Gideon and to Samuel.[16] The former led his people when a leader was required, but refused to perpetuate his rule; the latter opposed the selfishness of kings. Jesus is defending disinterestedness, not otherworldliness.

In defining intellectual virtue, Jesus does reject the seeking of glory (3. 100–107), but in citing Scipio, whose service to his country was vitiated by his motive, Jesus indicates that the object of his attack is impurity in idealism. The rejection of glory is further qualified by Jesus' assertion that men who do not seek glory receive it (3. 142–44). Though Jesus does contrast worldly fame with divine approval (3. 47–70), there is nothing especially ascetic about the notion that it is better to do what is right than what is popular: Jesus stresses the false values of the majority of men (3. 49–51) and honors the approval of the "singularly good," the "intelligent," and the "wise" (3. 57–59). There is no "fanatical otherworldliness" [17] in the poem's values; Jesus rejects not money, politics, and fame, but avarice, despotism, and vanity. The rejections are made in behalf of self-control, disinterested moral instruction, and humble faith: the values are not negative ones.

Formulating the poem's "true theme," James Hanford sums up its action: "as mankind fell through Adam's weakness, it stands again in Christ's firm resistance of the characteristic temptations of human life." [18] Approached in terms of its three main divisions, the retrospective portion of Jesus' first soliloquy provides an exposition for this action. The divisions correlate with the coming tests. The last section is directly related to the later debates concerning God's prophecies — to Jesus' intellectual trials — and the third day's conjunction of courage and holiness is anticipated in Jesus' reaction to the messiah's sacrificial role (1. 263–69): "neither . . . disheartened or dismayed,/ The time prefixed I waited." The second section of the speech relates to the second temptation. Not only are the sorts of rule which Jesus contemplates connected with the offers and rejections of the second day, but Jesus' interest in the Law anticipates Satan's offer of learning, and the disputation with the rabbis by which Jesus remembers his youthful aptitude is the hint by which Satan formulates his offer (4. 212–21). The brief opening section completes the pattern, for Jesus' indifference to "childish play" (1. 201–2) suggests the virtue of temperance.

The three divisions correlate with the faculties, then, and the fact that learning is subordinated to doing ("all my mind was set/ Serious to learn and know, and thence to do/ What might be public good" [1. 202–4]) agrees with the values of the poem: the virtue assigned to the reason is justice, the ruler's virtue. But the faculties are connected here with time. Sense is linked with childhood, of course. Reason is connected with boyhood: Jesus' dispute with the rabbis preceded by a year his arrival at manhood, and his thoughts of rule were apparently contemporaneous (there is no suggestion of a change of time in the introductory phrases: "Yet this not all/ To which my spirit aspired," "Yet held it more humane" [1. 214–15, 221]). Intellect is correlated with manhood. Mary's revelation followed "soon" after Jesus' thoughts of rule (1. 227–28), and the fact that the revelation deals with parentage suggests that the moment chosen was Jesus' coming of age, the appropriate moment for such a revelation. The sequence represents the natural unfolding of the faculties in order from lowest to highest. The retrospective portion of the soliloquy, then, indicates that Jesus has arrived at a mature and perfect state, a state like that which theological tradition assigns to Adam at the time of his creation; the test which follows is thus a parallel to Adam's test.

Jesus' initial perfection precludes the sort of growth assigned to the fallen Adam in *Paradise Lost*. The potentiality for change which Milton attributes to Jesus in only the freedom to lapse: though perfect, Jesus is limited, and so can fall. Although Jesus' faith is not defective, his knowledge of his role of savior is incomplete. The scale of ignorance which precedes the second temptation is anticipated in the scene of Jesus' arrival in the desert; there Jesus wonders "How best the mighty work he might begin/ Of Saviour to mankind" (1. 185–88). Since the third day's trial does not provide answers to this question, the point of the deficiency is not that Jesus has room to grow, but that he is susceptible to the sort of challenges which Satan offers, the exhortations to "fulfill" and "verify/ The Prophets old" (3. 177–78) which culminate in Satan's proposal that Jesus "Cast [him]self down, safely if Son of God" (4. 554–59).

Although Jesus has nothing to learn about the nature of rule, there are points of potential failure in his early resolutions. His wish to "rescue Israel" and to "subdue and quell o'er all the earth . . . proud tyrannic pow'r" (1. 216–20) suggests that he might forget his "more humane, more heavenly" conception of rule, and the fact that his mind was "set . . . to learn . . . and thence to do/ What might be public good" suggests that he could be distracted from doing by the opportunity of learning. Satan attacks at both these points. Finally, after the trial of sense, Jesus is faced with a new sensory hardship, hunger. The possibility of failure is suggested by Jesus' plaintive "Where will this end?" (2. 245). Denied the patterning of growth in *Paradise Regained*, Milton uses the pattern of trial and reward. Jesus succeeds where

Adam failed, is vindicated by God's rescue, and is rewarded in the angelic banquet which follows his final victory.

The action of *Paradise Regained* is the proving of Jesus, then, but critics have questioned whether the protagonist's struggle is more than merely nominal. The question involves the problem of Jesus' nature. If Jesus has that dual nature which is conventionally attributed to the incarnate Son, then he is impervious to human temptations; in fact, Elizabeth Pope demonstrates, many exegetes were driven to the conclusion that Christ temporarily laid aside divine consciousness in order to undergo trial.[19] Jackson Cope is the most extreme of the critics who assert the orthodoxy of Milton's Jesus: he claims that *Paradise Regained* is ritualistic rather than dramatic.[20] The view of George Whiting is more typical. Claiming that the Jesus of *Paradise Regained* is "both the perfect man and the Son of God," Whiting concludes that the poem is "essentially undramatic": "Christ's humanity and weakness are only superficial. . . . Secure in his consummate virtue, he easily vanquishes Satan and his solicitations." [21]

Whiting argues the divinity of Milton's Jesus from Jesus' "consci-ous[ness] of his divine birth and his divine mission," from his prepara-tion to undergo trials in the wilderness, from the divine proclamation of his baptism,[22] and especially from his miraculous fast: Protestant theologians, he says, denying that Christ's fast was a human act to be imitated by the pious, argued that it was evidence of his divinity.[23] Whiting's evidence better proves Jesus' humanity than his divinity. Jesus has no memory of his Sonship or of the Son's chosen mission: Mary revealed the facts of the miraculous conception, the Bible's prophecies informed him of his mission (1. 227–67). He has no divine foreknowledge, for he does not know what will befall him in the wilder-ness (1. 290–92). He has no superhuman prerogatives: God proclaims his Sonship, God sustains him in the wilderness (2. 247–51)—he does not choose the time to begin his mission among men (1. 280–89), he is not exempt from human hunger and does not sustain himself miraculously.

The function of the revelations of Jesus' divinity is not to prove him superhuman, as Whiting suggests, but to provide Jesus with human intellectual trials. Jesus must trust his belief that he is the predicted messiah (1. 259–63)—must trust "What from within [he] feel[s] [him]-self" (1. 198)—and he must accept the faith of the "new-baptized" (2. 1–6) and credit the revelations made to Mary, Simeon, Anna, and John the Baptist (1. 234–58, 274–79)—must accept "What from with-out comes often to [his] ears" (1. 199)—even though the Sonship he believes in is "Ill sorting with [his] present state compared" (1. 200). In this, Jesus is like every man (given of course the theological outlook of the poem). Every man must believe in God's favor and in his revealed mysteries, however unlikely these seem to the empirical eye.

Though Miss Pope, unlike Whiting, believes that Milton portrays Jesus as a human being,[24] she nevertheless suggests that Milton writes "under the influence" of the tradition that Christ, divine, deliberately withheld evidences of his identity from the devil.[25] The premise of Miss Pope's argument is that Milton is trying to re-create the Christ of the Gospels. Finding that Milton does not attribute to Jesus the attributes which, she says, "we expect any writer with the least feeling for Christianity to attribute to him," [26] she calls upon the tradition to account for the flaws she finds in the rendering: the negativity in Jesus' definitions of his goals, his use of internal disproof rather than of alternative proposals, and his impersonal statement of what positive definitions he makes.

The problem with Miss Pope's argument is its premise: comparing the figure in the poem to the figure in the Bible, she neglects to examine the function of particular arguments in the poem. Sometimes therefore she misses the exact point of the passages she cites. Referring to Jesus' statement that the means to his kingdom are "not for [Satan] to know or [him] to tell" (4. 152–53), she asks why Jesus should not declare the "form [his kingdom] is to take" and "in what way he proposes to reign over it." [27] Jesus makes clear elsewhere that he means to rule not "the body" but the "inner man" (2. 473–80); this particular argument is concerned with a different question, however, the question of the implementation of God's prophecies. Jesus is not withholding what he knows, as Miss Pope supposes, but asserting both his ignorance and his faith.[28] Miss Pope complains that, denouncing the mob in his rejection of glory, Jesus does not "assert[ ] that he intends to raise [the masses] to the level that they will applaud the good." [29] But Jesus is contrasting expediency with absolute values, earthly with divine judgment; a statement of social duty would be irrelevant to the argument.

In another instance Miss Pope misses the argumentative appropriateness of Jesus' reply. When she complains that Jesus does not say that he will "bestow" upon the Romans a liberty "greater than mere physical emanicipation can be," [30] she fails to see that by confining himself to the faults in Satan's offer, Jesus is bringing the discussion of kingdoms to a close, refusing in specific terms what he sees to be Satan's final bait.[31] Finally, decrying the impersonality of Jesus' defini-

tions of true glory (3. 89–93) and true leadership (3. 473–76),[32] Miss
Pope misses the premise which underlies the second day's trial, that
Jesus must give reasoned replies, and thus must make general rather
than personal statements. Judged in their context, Jesus' replies are
skillful and well reasoned, not reticent and evasive; thus there is no
need to suppose Milton influenced by a tradition which posits Jesus'
divine consciousness.

A special version of the theory that Jesus has a dual nature has been
broached by Allen, elaborated and systematized by Mrs. Lewalski.
Refining Allen's theory that Jesus "crosses and recrosses the boundary
between the two persons" of his dual nature,[33] Mrs. Lewalski claims
that by his unaided virtuous responses Jesus earns intermittent divine
revelations.[34] There are problems of evidence with this view. First of
all, the instances of illumination which these critics cite are unconvincing. Claiming that Jesus "not only knows himself, but remembers the
long history of his opponent both in Heaven and in earth," [35] Allen
refers to Jesus' depiction of Satan's arrival in heaven before his trial
of Job, and to Jesus' subsequent account of Satan's influence on men
(1. 410–40).

Even Mrs. Lewalski rejects this reading, claiming that Jesus' striking
description is his "imaginative re-creation" of events recounted in
Job; [36] the subsequent history can be similarly explained. The reason
for Mrs. Lewalski's objection is, apparently, that Allen's reading en-
dangers the theory that Jesus becomes increasingly conscious of his
divinity: such extensive recollections make his knowledge complete
from the start. Mrs. Lewalski finds a more limited illustration later in
the same speech. Arguing that Milton places the cessation of pagan
oracles not at the birth of Jesus but at his baptism, she takes "henceforth oracles are ceased" (1. 456) as Jesus' announcement of a divine
intention newly revealed to him. In "God hath now sent his living
Oracle/ Into the world" (1. 460–61), Jesus—she claims—receives a
special revelation about his prophetic office.[37] Now it is possible to
take Jesus' prediction as simply the invocation of a text in Micah, "thou
shalt have no more soothsayers"; [38] Jesus expects the fulfillment of
messianic prophecies.

But in fact Milton may be honoring rather than altering the tradition
concerning the cessation of oracles. Jesus may be basing his prediction
on a silence at Delphi already of some thirty years' duration, in which
case "this thy glory soon shall be retrenched" (1. 454) refers to the
passing of Satan's rites, his "pomp and sacrifice" (1. 457): "henceforth
oracles are ceased" would predict the perpetuity of silence, rather than

announce its commencement. Even without this reading, there is no need to posit illumination, nor is revelation needed to explain why Jesus calls himself a "living Oracle." Jesus has already decided that he is to rule by "winning words," and the subject of prophecy leads naturally to his selection of the metaphor of the oracle at this particular point.

The other instances are even less persuasive. Professors Allen and Lewalski both claim that Jesus receives divine insight in replying to the offer of the banquet (2. 378–91); [39] Mrs. Lewalski argues that in "I can . . . command a table" Jesus "asserts . . . lordship over nature as the Creator and Son of God." Jesus' reply may be argumentative rather than declarative, however; Miss Pope glosses it thus: "If I *am* the Son of God, as you say that I am, with power over the resources of the world, then why should you trouble yourself to see my needs satisfied, when according to your own argument, I can have whatever I like merely by ordering it?" [40]

These two readings differ in their interpretation of Jesus' rhetorical questions: "Said'st thou not . . . ?" "And who withholds my pow'r . . . ?" "Shall I receive by gift . . . ?" "Why shouldst thou . . . obtrude . . . ?" If the speech is assertive, the rhetorical questions are indignant reproaches; if the speech is argumentative, the questions are mild rebuttals, logical examinations. When Milton says that Jesus replies "temperately" (2. 378), he rules out the possibility that Jesus is answering with what Mrs. Lewalski calls "ringing certitude and challenge." [41] Jesus' argument is both less evasive and more subtle and witty than Miss Pope sees (she overlooks the functions of the biblical allusions),[42] but she is right in claiming that the speech is a logical reply to Satan's argument. Addressing Jesus as "Son of God" (2. 368, 377), Satan gives him inappropriate advice; Jesus replies by explaining what befits the Son of God.

Finally, Mrs. Lewalski argues that when Jesus, rejecting the offer of Rome, compares his kingdom to a world-overshadowing tree (4. 146–51), he is recounting a divine revelation; she claims that he "lay[s] claim to full knowledge of the means to his kingdom" when he tells Satan, "Means there shall be to this, but what the means/ Is not for thee to know, nor me to tell" (4. 152–54).[43] Since in like situations Jesus has refused to speculate on what "The Father in his purpose hath decreed" (3. 184–86), it is less likely that Jesus is boasting his secret knowledge here than that he is asserting a humble faith. As to the illumination itself, if Milton were portraying a Jesus who had only human sources of knowledge, he would attribute to him statements which could be traced to word-of-mouth or to reading; he would suggest supernatural instruction by assigning Jesus unknowable truths and unique imagery. The fact that Jesus' prediction paraphrases an Old Testament prophecy suggests that Milton is not rendering the receipt of some new communication. This conclusion is bolstered by the fact that the image from Daniel draws together earlier allusions by Jesus: Jesus is concluding old arguments, not announcing new revelations.[44]

Not only are the instances of illumination dubious, but the claim that the poem posits this kind of divine communication is doubtful. The chief evidence is of course Jesus' statement that "what concerns [his] knowledge God reveals" (1. 293); Mrs. Lewalski interprets it as Jesus' assertion that illumination is available to him.[45] The passage of which the statement is a part (1. 290–93) resembles Jesus' second soliloquy (2. 245–59) in form and substance. In form, both passages are pious refusals to murmur. As Jesus finds himself hungry but provides himself reasons to ignore the hunger, so, reviewing his life, Jesus emerges from his reverie to find himself lost in the wilderness. Resigning himself to God's will, he argues that either he is seeking to know what God wishes to conceal, or he is seeking legitimate knowledge prematurely. "[W]hat concerns my knowledge God reveals" is a concluding expression of faith in God's favor. The statement says nothing at all about the way in which God communicates. One function of Jesus' second soliloquy is to show his susceptibility to sensory temptation (Professors Allen and Lewalski agree that Jesus shows human limitations here — they in fact exaggerate his frailty.) [46] The framing sections of the first soliloquy show Jesus' susceptibility to intellectual temptation. The speech is preceded by the description of Jesus' uncertainty about how to begin his work as savior. His opening exclamation, "O what a multitude of thoughts at once/ Awakened in me swarm" (1. 196–97) parallels the human frailty of "Where will this end?" The disparity between his declared state and his actual one causes Jesus to think about the unfolding of his life, and he returns to the present only to find a new cause of puzzlement, that God has led him into a pathless desert. The human limitations revealed here make unlikely the suggestion that Jesus is confident of special superhuman prerogatives.

Jesus' changes of tone are the second major evidence of illumination: both proponents interpret these changes as signs of inspiration. Allen exclaims, "how strongly the undefined expectations of the human Christ flare into divine certainty whenever he is confronted by the subhuman enticements of the mind of evil," [47] and Mrs. Lewalski,

endorsing this view,[48] contrasts the "certitude" of Jesus' pronouncement on oracles with his "doubts and hesitations" earlier,[49] and argues
that his "matter-of-fact response to the banquet offer . . . modulates
at length to ringing certitude and challenge as he seems to receive
another . . . divine illumination[ ]." [50] Yet (even granting all the examples—and the last is dubious), if Jesus becomes more firm in the
presence of Satan, he only responds like Milton's Samson, who is
roused from despondency and brought to certainty by the lures and
challenges of Dalila and Harapha. Certainty need not be taken as
evidence of divine power: it is, after all, as human as hesitancy.

Mrs. Lewalski chooses between differing views of Jesus' nature on
the basis of what provides "a genuine dramatic action," [51] and she
praises Allen's reading because it is a "dramatic" one.[52] Yet the sort
of drama which these critics propose undermines the poem as surely
as Whiting's undramatic reading. Even the terms of combat as Mrs.
Lewalski describes them sound suspicious. "In this conflict," she says,
"Satan's special advantage will be his firsthand acquaintance with the
accumulated knowledge and experience of history, his direct observation of human motives and human weaknesses throughout all time,
whereas Christ knows such things only at second hand, through his
wide reading in the scriptural and historical records. But more than
compensating for this is Christ's special advantage, the gift of divine
illumination which he may merit, whereas Satan can rely only upon
his own brilliant but now warped intellect." [53] Jesus' advantage, it
seems, is not to be the moral advantage of a virtuous mind, but the
external aid of an infallible prompter. The doubts aroused by the
terms are borne out by the events. According to Allen, Jesus is at first
full of "undefined expectations," but he is "raised above humanity"
during his pronouncement on oracles. After his "ecstacy," he returns
to an "uncertain, unknowing" state: hungry, he longs for the divine
aid pictured in his dream, although "he does not admit it." During the
subsequent banquet scene, however, Jesus' "Godliness" is again
"made manifest." [54] Mrs. Lewalski's account is slightly more cautious.
Jesus' initial state is one of "doubts and hesitations," she says, but "by
withstanding [the] first temptation directed at his prophetic office,"
Jesus "merit[s]" a "special revelation regarding this office." [55] Afterward, left alone, he reverts "to the state of simple human vulnerability
and uncertainty," [56] but during the banquet scene his "matter-of-fact
response" gives way to a sureness which is evidence of divine revelation.[57]

In both these accounts, Jesus as a human being is weak—in Allen's account almost sinfully weak; he is morally impressive only when his divine nature is supplied with God's hidden knowledge. Mrs. Lewalski, it is true, says that Jesus' unaided human efforts merit these revelations, but the events as she describes them speak for themselves. Twice God intervenes with indecent haste, bestowing rewards after a single opening encounter; and though Jesus is roused by the aid, he sinks into weakness when left to his own resources. *Paradise Regained* shows, then, how God, having boasted to his angels that a "perfect man" of "consummate virtue" would defeat Satan (1. 155–67), bestowed victory on him by supplementing his human powers with supernatural ones. Satan's comment is apt: "What will he not do to advance his Son?" (1. 88).

Mankind, which "fell through Adam's weakness, . . . stands again in Christ's firm resistance of the characteristic temptations of human life": as Hanford's formulation of the "theme" implies, Milton, who takes his tripartite division of sins from the tradition of the triple equation, also refers repeatedly to its comparison of Christ with Adam and Eve. These references are not, as Miss Pope believes, the "natural" and "inevitable" result of Milton's writing a "sequel and companionpiece to *Paradise Lost,"* [58] for in his audacious opening line, "I who erewhile the happy garden sung," Milton warns the reader to expect not a sequel but a work as different from *Paradise Lost* as epic is from pastoral. The two poems are not compatible. Not only do they divide and group their theological materials in different ways,[59] but there is no continuity of character between them.

As E. M. W. Tillyard says, the Satan of *Paradise Regained* is "so different from his namesake in *Paradise Lost* that it is a pity he cannot be given another title." [60] More important, the works are so different in their mode of organization that a reader who approaches *Paradise Regained* expecting the dramatic richness of *Paradise Lost* will leave feeling cheated. By likening Jesus to Adam and Eve, Milton is not evoking his earlier poem but recalling a theological tradition. Yet, though Milton makes straightforward conceptual use of the tripartite division of sins, he does not make this sort of use of the comparisons. Conventionally, as Miss Pope demonstrates, the temptations of flesh, world, and devil are paired with Eve's gluttony, desire for knowledge, and desire for godhood.[61] Milton does treat the second pair conventionally. He does not treat the third conventionally, but an ingenious man could view Milton's treatment as a necessary adaptation to his stress on Satan's violence. Milton substitutes for an allusion to Eve's pride a distant reference to God's curse (4. 585), evoking—at two removes—Eve's cowardly excuse ("The serpent beguiled me, and I did eat"), contrasting it with Jesus' courageous faith.

But Milton's unconventional treatment of the first correspondence defies rationalization. Milton mentions Eve's apple only in connection with the offer of the world (2. 348–49), and even if, as Allen supposes,[62] Satan makes a glancing reference to Adam's lust (2. 134)—lust is of course the parallel to Eve's gluttony—Milton makes no authorial mention of the sin. The point of comparison which Milton selects is Satan's use of disguise. Eve did not question the talking serpent, but Jesus detects Satan's "grey dissimulation" (1. 498): "thus answered th' Arch-Fiend, now undisguised" (1. 357). The linking is an incidental one, for disguise does not bear on man's appetitive sin, nor is it the mark of Jesus' first trial: Satan does not abandon human guise until the last day.[63]

Milton is not interested in exact moral correspondences, then; he cares only to balance Jesus' success against the failure of Adam and Eve. After Jesus' refusal to turn stones into bread, he recalls the weakness of Eve, and he alludes to Eve again before the offer of Rome:

> Perplexed and troubled at his bad success
> The tempter stood, nor had what to reply,
> Discovered in his fraud, thrown from his hope,
> So oft, and the persuasive rhetoric
> That sleeked his tongue, and won so much on Eve,
> So little here, yea lost; but Eve was Eve,
> This far his overmatch, who, self-deceived
> And rash, beforehand had no better weighed
> The strength he was to cope with, or his own.
>   (4. 1–9)

Jesus is an "overmatch" for Satan as Satan was for Eve, and as Eve was foolish, so is Satan now: "self-deceived" and "rash" recall the rational weaknesses which tradition assigns to women.[64] Concluding the tower scene, Milton juxtaposes Satan's fall and Jesus' reception by the angels (4. 581–85). In the description of Jesus, the fulfillment of the psalmist's pledge invoked by Satan ("it is written, 'He will give command concerning thee to his angels'") (4. 556–59) is combined with a second allusion, an allusion to the promise in Isaiah that the faithful "shall rest in their beds": [65] the angels' wings form a "floating couch" for Jesus. What Isaiah promises is the reversal of the curses of labor, pain, and death visited upon disobedient mankind. The passage contrasts Satan with Jesus: Satan "f[a]ll[s]" while Jesus is "up-

bor[ne]." The antithesis suggests that Satan's fall has a twofold meaning. In reference to the invitation that Jesus "Cast [him]self down,"
"Satan fell" means "instead of causing Jesus to fall, Satan descended
to hell." But in reference to the fall of man—evoked by the text in
Isaiah—"Satan fell" means "instead of bringing ruin to mankind, Satan was destroyed."

The meaning of Milton's repeated comparisons of Jesus to Adam
and Eve is told in the poem's argument, where the motif appears for
the first time:

> I who erewhile the happy garden sung
> By one man's disobedience lost, now sing
> Recovered Paradise to all mankind,
> By one man's firm obedience fully tried
> Through all temptation, and the Tempter foiled
> In all his wiles, defeated and repulsed,
> And Eden raised in the waste wilderness.
>
> (1. 1–7)

Milton announces that he is treating Jesus' victory not as God's defeat
of the devil but as a human victory which balances man's initial lapse.
The places where Milton repeats the motif are crucial points in the
temptations: Jesus' refusal to turn stones into bread is the central
incident of the first day, the offer of Rome the most characteristic offer
of the second day, the tower scene the climactic episode of the third
day. At each stage of Jesus' victory, Milton recalls what sort of victory
it is. The motif from the triple equation is used, then, to announce and
to emphasize the humanity of the protagonist of *Paradise Regained.*
Jesus is—as Stein and Frye have observed [66]—a perfect but limited
and fallible being, the second Adam. (There is no evidence for the
qualification which both these critics add, that Jesus is transformed
into a deity at the end of the poem.) [67]

By adopting the view that the incarnation was accomplished by an
"emptying out by the divine nature of that which properly belongs to
itself as divine" (the description is Mrs. Lewalski's),[68] Milton gains the
advantage of a real struggle between his central characters. Jesus is
not a deity pretending to be human or a human being supplied with
superhuman powers, he is a mere man, subject to temptation and able
to fall. Milton exploits this advantage. He uses the angels to suggest
the precariousness of Jesus' position, and Jesus' followers to indicate
the importance of the outcome. When he demonstrates that Jesus is
vulnerable, he covers not only the broad points, but the details as well.

Before Satan's description of the rigors of the wilderness (1. 321–25, 337–41) he shows that Jesus is actually lost (1. 294–98), and before the storm he describes him as "Hungry and cold" (4. 403)—in a weakened physical condition. Before the shepherd's request for a miracle (1. 342–43) he indicates that Jesus has no forewarning of Satan's approach: Jesus enters the desert ignorant of his coming trials (1. 290–94), and he spends the following days mulling over his first day's topics—"things past and to come" (1. 299–302). Furthermore, Milton is careful to show that only human processes of mind are involved in Jesus' victories. Jesus overcomes the trials of his sensory soul because he cannot be cajoled, lured, or frightened into intemperance. He succeeds in his rational trials because (as his indirect argumentation proves) he is alert to fallacious reasoning, and because he understands clearly his duties to other men. He can repel the assaults on his intellect because he trusts God and is loyal to the death. By stressing the humanity of Jesus, Milton holds open the possibility of his defeat.

The final question about the dramatic structure of *Paradise Regained* is the relation of Satan's story to Jesus'. But before this large question can be settled, a smaller one must be decided, a question raised by the problem of Satan's motivation. As Miss Pope shows, theologians disagreed as to whether the devil wished to learn Christ's identity or whether, knowing, he wished to subvert him.[69] Critics have assigned to Milton's Satan one or the other aim, or both aims. The two extreme positions are represented by Professors Lewalski and Allen, who, agreeing that the action of *Paradise Regained* is Jesus' recovery of his divine identity, choose different means of integrating Satan's motives with that action. Mrs. Lewalski straightforwardly claims that "a puzzled and deluded Satan" is "seeking throughout the temptation to learn whether Christ is indeed divine." [70] Satan's primary quest, to learn Jesus' identity, parallels Jesus' journey to the realization of that identity. Allen more intricately argues that Satan knows that Jesus is divine, that his "uncertainty is really a pretense" for "heartening his colleagues" and "establish[ing] a mood of self-distrust in the mind of the exalted man." [71] Satan's initial certainty is thus balanced against Jesus' initial uncertainty. There are problems of evidence with both these views. Many of Satan's references to Jesus' Sonship are not, as Mrs. Lewalski supposes, real doubts, but, as Allen argues, temptations. On the other hand, the major references to Jesus' identity cannot be disposed of so easily as Allen believes.

There is, first of all, no evidence that Satan has what Allen calls "diplomatic reasons" [72] for the doubts he first expresses to his followers. After his sober background narrative (1. 44–65), Satan recounts the proclamations of Jesus' Sonship, concluding that the identity of Jesus must be ascertained (1. 66–93); then he states a second aim, to subvert Jesus "Ere in the head of nations he appear" (1. 94–99). Closing with the announcement that he himself will undertake the mission, he introduces a note of optimism, recalling the success of his "expedition to find out/ And ruin Adam" (1. 100–105). The placement of the statement of doubt—between the gloomy opening and the announcement of the "danger" posed by Jesus' kingship—suggests that Satan is expressing an actual worry: his attempt to hearten comes later, and entails a shift in tone. The fact that Satan speaks "With looks aghast and sad" (1. 43), furthermore, does not suggest that he is concealing misgivings in order to hearten his followers; and even his final optimism is real. For were it feigned, Satan would maintain the pose after his first defeat. Instead he repudiates his earlier assurance (2. 140–46).

The reply to Jesus' indignant "Get thee behind me" (4. 170–97) is the second major passage in which Satan expresses uncertainty about Jesus' nature: "Be not so sore offended, Son of God,/ Though sons of God both angels are and men" (4. 196–208). Allen groups the speech with the "sly doubts" of Satan's temptations,[73] but the situation here is an extraordinary one. Satan has just given vent to his anger (4. 154–69), Jesus has rebuked him, and Satan is afraid of losing his opportunity to tempt. Speaking "with fear abashed" (4. 195), he offers an excuse, that he was "try[ing]" Jesus, and so performing his permitted role (4. 174–75), the role of tempter. He puts his temptation in the best light possible: he was not seeking to subvert Jesus, but merely to learn his identity (Jesus has just pointedly reminded him of the question [4. 175–81]). Only after this excuse does Satan resume his usual tempter's role: "Therefore let pass, as they are transitory,/ The kingdoms of this world" (4. 209 ff.).

If Satan were expressing a doubt of Jesus' nature in order to tempt, then his doubt could be discounted; but there is no temptation here. Satan's excuse is false in one way (he was not trying Jesus but expressing his rage) [74] and therefore it could be false in another (he has no question about Jesus' identity), yet Milton does not attribute so much aplomb to Satan here: Satan is upset, not sly. The interpretation which accords best with the situation as a whole is that, cornered, Satan is revealing a part of his intent in order to save the rest—that in order to preserve the opportunity and cover the intention to corrupt, Satan is exposing a real if secondary concern.

Allen disposes of the genuineness of Satan's doubts by what is essentially a deductive argument. He argues that Satan learns Jesus' divinity from his words during the first encounter: "Knowing who I am, as I know who thou art" (1. 356). Later, however, Satan persists in his claim of ignorance: Adam, he tells his council, is "to this man inferior far,/ If he be man by mother's side at least" (2. 129–39). Since the later claim is false, Allen deduces, the earlier statements must also be disingenious.[75] The fault lies in Allen's supposition that Jesus is claiming to recognize the Son's heavenly antagonist: the theory posits not only that Jesus have an extraordinarily complete flash of divine memory, but that Satan disguise himself as an aged and wingless but still recognizable archangel. It is easier to suppose that Jesus identifies Satan by deduction, recognizing the evil under the shepherd's seeming simplicity. In this case, Satan would learn nothing positive about Jesus' relationship to the Son, and later could express doubt truthfully.

If neither of the extreme positions is valid, Stein's intermediate view of Satan's motivation must be correct: Satan has the primary aim of subverting Jesus and the "lesser aim" of determining Jesus' identity.[76] But the relationship of the "lesser aim" to the action needs to be explained, for it is not obvious, like the relation of subversion to the testing of Jesus. The key lies in two early considerations of Jesus' Sonship, Satan's discussion and Jesus' own retrospective meditation. Jesus reviews the testimonies concerning his identity—the prophecies and the Father's declaration—and accepts what God has revealed, while Satan, present when the Father acknowledged his Son, refuses to credit what is empirically unlikely: "man he seems/ In all his lineaments" (1. 91–92). The differing spiritual states are epitomized in the contrasting accounts of Jesus' baptism. Both Satan and Jesus have access to the messianic text in Isaiah, "The spirit of the Lord shall rest upon him" [77] (the dove's descent is conventionally taken as the fulfillment of this prophecy). Jesus, faithful, believes the text: "The Spirit descended on me like a dove" (1. 282). Satan, unfaithful, is puzzled: "[I saw] A perfect dove descend, whate'er it meant" (1. 82–83). Satan's doubt of Jesus' identity is the antithesis to Jesus' faith in God's pronouncements, then. His "lesser aim" is part of a contrast of the evil intellect with the virtuous intellect, and this contrast is in turn part of the general antithesis of Satan and Jesus: Jesus exemplifies the rightful use of all the faculties, Satan their misuse.

As to the broader question of the relation of Satan's story to Jesus' story, Allen suggests that the two form a symmetrical opposition: "As Satan's fears increase and as he exhausts the quiver of the temptations, Christ's sense of his own divinity increases and the human side of his nature becomes more obscure." [78] This solution, though attractive, is untenable; it needs modification in two respects. First of all, Allen wrongly supposes that Satan regresses, that he loses his higher resources and is reduced to a "cornered and desperate animal." [79] In fact, Satan loses the lower resources first: his last resource is his perverted will, the highest faculty. Satan deteriorates, but he does not regress. Secondly, because Jesus does not develop—he is merely tested and rewarded—the contrast of his story with Satan's is less direct than Allen believes. Though Jesus' success and reward *are* contrasted with Satan's failure and punishment, the contrast is not a symmetrical one. The angelic banquet provides an external reward for Jesus, but Satan receives no external punishment. Satan's punishment is his progressive deterioration; he is punished internally, and it is significant that his story ends with a fall which—whatever its further meanings—is a realistically probable consequence of psychological exhaustion. Satan topples from the temple roof in surprise (4. 562), he is too full of "dread and anguish" to recover flight (4. 576), and, his will having been broken, he makes no new attempt.

The Power of Darkness,
the Power of the Son

MILTON'S CHOICE of values in *Paradise Regained* suggests his aim. Having drawn from the traditional triple equation the idea of three sins correlative with three faculties, Milton could have chosen the three theological virtues as antitheses to flesh, world, and devil. Instead he chose three virtues which Plato in the *Gorgias* identifies with harmony within the self, "what is proper . . . in relation . . . to men," and "what is proper in relation to the gods." The choice suggests that Milton was not satisfied with the exemplification of religiousness alone. Furthermore, having classified the virtues exhaustively by reference to the faculties, Milton did not need to stress Satan's violence, and to call up thereby the antithetical virtue of courage.

In the *Gorgias* Plato completes a classification of virtues according to their place of action, then adds a supernumerary virtue, courage. He does so in order to describe the "perfectly good man" by reference to the four cardinal virtues (here temperance, justice, holiness, and courage).[1] Apparently Milton included courage for a similar reason, to exemplify moral perfection by reference to the philosopher's list. The end of *Paradise Regained,* then, is to exemplify the "perfectly good man": who readeth Aeneas carrying old Anchises on his back that wisheth not it were his fortune to perform so excellent an act? The poem's sentiments are the primary vehicle to this end: intricacies of moral argument, not intricacies of character or plot, are the central means by which perfection is defined. Character and action serve to validate the sentiments: strong and weak arguments are correlated with admirable and contemptible agents; virtue is rewarded and evil punished.

The minor characters being much subordinated, the dramatic pattern of the poem consists almost entirely of the juxtaposition of the protagonist's nobility and success with the corruption and ruin of the antagonist. Jesus changes only in fortune: he faces increasingly difficult challenges without lapsing, then receives an external reward. Satan changes in character; he grows progressively feebler as he dedicates each of his capacities in turn to evil ends. The three sections of Jesus' trial coincide with the three stages of Satan's decline, and as the poem's schematic structure is notable for its varied treatment of similar elements, so the dramatic structure is handled with virtuosity. In the first unit, the action is handled retrospectively. The second unit climaxes at its center, and climaxes at a point which receives little schematic stress. The third unit develops straightforwardly to a climactic close.

Satan's first address to his council serves as an exposition to his story, balancing the exposition provided by the central portion of Jesus' first soliloquy.[2] Like Jesus' remembrance of his boyhood (1. 206–26) and manhood (1. 227–89), Satan's statement of objectives prefigures the last two temptations. Satan's desire to learn Jesus' relation to the heavenly Son (1. 66–93) foreshadows the climactic episode of the third day, where, exploiting his desire to learn "what more . . . than man" Jesus is (4. 538), Satan tries to trap Jesus into an impious and fatal claim of godhood (4. 555–59). Satan's resolve to circumvent Jesus' appearance "in the head of nations" (1. 94–99) anticipates his use of worldly snares. As Jesus' memory of his childhood (1. 201–6) touches lightly upon the issues of the first temptation, Satan's announcement that he will undertake the trial of Jesus (1. 100–105) introduces the day's events: Satan's happy memory of his first expedition to earth accounts for his opening maneuver, his appeal to hunger. The retrospective section of Jesus' soliloquy reveals his growth to a mature human perfection. Antithetical to his years of growth are the ages of anticipation, worry, and dread which Satan recalls in the historical introduction to his speech (1. 44–65); the speech itself particularizes Satan's moral weaknesses. Satan's incredulity that the mortal Jesus could be the heavenly Son contrasts with Jesus' faith in the identity God has declared. Jesus' careful consideration of ruling shows the superficiality of Satan's thoughtless equation of rule with heroic conquest. That the assumption springs from a corrupt reason is suggested by Satan's concomitant decision to use sophistry as a weapon, "well-couched fraud, well-woven snares" (1. 97). (When, on the third day, rational corruption has yielded to rational exhaustion, Satan, incapable of argument, turns from fraud to force.) In assuming the tempter's mission, Satan reveals his sensory weaknesses. The sudden lightening of mood at the end of his gloomy speech suggests Satan's lack of temperate self-control, and the gratification of the senses informs Satan's closing imagery of travel: "a calmer voyage now/ Will waft me; and the way found prosperous once/ Induces best to hope of like success" (1. 103–5). Comparing himself to a successful merchant-explorer, Satan displays the voyager's love of the sweet air, and the trader's love of gain. Satan's laxity is of course the opposite of Jesus' childhood strictness.

The introduction to the banquet scene (2. 235–84) establishes that Jesus has not been shaken by Satan's first attack, his attack on the sensory soul. The exclamation of distress which opens the second soliloquy (2. 245–59) — "Where will this end?" — shows that Jesus is susceptible to physical suffering; hunger is visited upon him to test whether the first day's trials have impaired his self-control. His resolve to ignore the "sting of famine" for the "better thoughts" which "feed/ [Him] hungering to do [his] Father's will" recalls Jesus' childhood seriousness to learn, do, and promote "all righteous things" (1. 202–6): both statements describe the subordination of the senses. The echo of the first soliloquy suggests that Jesus has not been affected by the intervening assault. Jesus' resolution to remain content so long as hunger does not waste him parallels — though here there is no surface likeness — his childhood indifference to play (1. 201–2). the resolve shows that Jesus has not succumbed to self-indulgence. Jesus' dream (2. 266–78) proves that his temperance is more than verbal. Like the cry of distress in the soliloquy, the fact that Jesus dreams "as appetite is wont to dream" (2. 264) demonstrates his susceptibility to human appetites. But Don Cameron Allen exaggerates the frailty displayed: Jesus' dream is not, as Allen says, a plea for divine intervention,[3] it is a confirmation of Jesus' temperate words. Jesus' contentment with simple subsistence is corroborated by his dreamed dinner of pulse and of such portions as the ravens brought Elijah; the dreamed company of Elijah and of Daniel proves that Jesus does value "better thoughts" above mere food. The scene stresses Jesus' self-control — self-control so great that even when the reason is relaxed in sleep, the fancy does not revel in excess. As Arnold Stein says, the incident is "an image of perfect temperance, in which the unconscious has been so permeated by the conscious that even the dreams are pure." [4]

The sensory ruin which befalls Satan as a result of the first temptation is rendered in Satan's irritable depression on the second day:
depression, as apathy, is suggestive of emotional death, and temper,
as loss of self-control, suggests the death of passional virtue. The
second induction to the second day (2. 115–241) has as one of its
purposes the backward glance to the first day: the introduction to the
banquet shows Jesus' unchanged state, and Satan's second council
introduces and accounts for Satan's change. As Stein has noted, the
episode is treated comically.[5] Concluding his introductory remarks (2.
140–46), Satan repudiates the hopeful words with which he ended the
first assembly:

> I am returned, lest confidence
> Of my success with Eve in Paradise
> Deceive ye to persuasion over-sure
> Of like succeeding here; I summon all
> Rather to be in readiness, with hand
> Or counsel to assist.

There is comedy in the way that Satan glosses over his own previous
self-confidence, his own expectation of an easy second seduction of
mankind (1. 100–105):

> I, when no other durst, sole undertook
> The dismal expedition to find out
> And ruin Adam, and the exploit performed
> Successfully: a calmer voyage now
> Will waft me.

Satan's sensuousness—it is revealed in the voyage imagery of the
first day's speech—is repudiated in the second day's debate, in Satan's
surprising puritanical rejoinder to doting Belial (2. 173–224). The two
repudiations suggest that in the interval since the first assembly Satan
has suffered a collapse, and the comic treatment helps designate the
area of change: the absurdity and embarassment assigned to Satan are
usual and fitting wages of passional transgression. As Stein has observed, Satan's rebuttal of Belial—his disparagement of feminine wiles
—is related to his preceding confrontation with Jesus.[6] Having argued
with feminine emotiveness—having begged for charity and for sympathy, having reproached and fawned—Satan feels like a rejected

beauty himself, "put to rout," his "pride deject" and "turn[ed] to reverent awe." Embarassment accounts for the excessive disdain which he heaps on Belial's excessive laxness. The passage thus serves to connect the exhaustion of Satan's sensory soul with his sensory trial of Jesus—the ruin of the faculty with its abuse.

The offer of Israel is an unemphatic offer; beginning his presentation of specific kingdoms, Satan thinks that his best baits are still to come, the two realms for which he reserves his "airy microscope" (4. 57). At the end of what had promised to be a quiet episode comes the dramatic climax of the second temptation—a sudden shift in the stances of the two central characters. The victim takes the offensive (3. 198–202). Answering Satan's exhortation to "zeal" (3. 171–72), Jesus repeats his argument that Satan's "gifts" are "guiles" (2. 391), but now he inverts the image. Instead of citing the advice of Proverbs on accepting a ruler's "deceitful meat," [7] Jesus speaks as a righteous ruler to a treacherous guest: "Why art thou/ Solicitous, what moves thy inquisition?" Jesus replies to Satan's appeal to "duty" (3. 171–72) by asserting that his own "rising" is Satan's "fall." Not only does he define the sort of rule which he intends—the freeing of men from Satan's deceits—but he takes up that rule, speaking as the teacher of a negligent student: "Know'st thou not . . . ?" Twice, then, Jesus speaks as "Israel's true king" (3. 441), and (as Barbara Lewalski has observed) [8] his pronouncements form an unprecedented direct challenge to Satan.

Taken at face value, the opening section of Satan's reply (3. 204–22) is a cry of remorse. First Satan states his hopelessness and accepts his destruction:

> Let that [my "destruction"] come when it comes; all hope is
>   lost
> Of my reception into grace; what worse?
> For where is left no hope, is left no fear.
> If there be worse, the expectation more
> Of worse torments me than the feeling can.
> I would be at the worst; worst is my port,
> My harbor and my ultimate repose,
> The end I would attain, my final good.

Grief is followed by guilt:

> My error was my error, and my crime
> My crime, whatever for itself condemned,

And will alike be punished, whether thou
Reign or reign not.

Just condemnation then leads Satan to think of the possibility of salvation, and addressing Jesus as the divine Son, he sees him as the savior, the being who protects the creature from his merited repudiation by the Father:

> though to that gentle brow
> Willingly I could fly, and hope thy reign,
> From that placid aspéct and meek regard,
> Rather than aggravate my evil state,
> Would stand between me and thy Father's ire
> (Whose ire I dread more than the fire of hell),
> A shelter and a kind of shading cool
> Interposition, as a summer's cloud.

The second section of the speech (3. 223–26) returns to the arguments of the offer of Israel:

> If I then to the worst that can be haste,
> Why move thy feet so slow to what is best,
> Happiest both to thyself and all the world,
> That thou who worthiest art should be their king?

The accusation of delay repeats Satan's reproach to Jesus for "sitting still" (3. 163–64). The parenthetical claim that Jesus would benefit himself repeats the exhortation that he show "zeal" for his father's house, and the assertion that Jesus would benefit others restates Satan's appeal to "duty." In defining "what is best," Satan refers to his reminder that Jesus is a destined king: "To a kingdom thou art born, ordained/ To sit upon thy father David's throne" (3. 152–53). The section opens with an explicit tie to the preceding one: Satan makes argumentative use of his desire for the "worst." But there are other, implicit ties as well. By urging Jesus' reign, Satan repudiates his guilty awareness that corrupting Jesus could not change his lot; and the sort of regal "worth" which Satan extols here is the reverse of the "placid[ity]" and "meek[ness]" which he had attributed to Jesus earlier. Alluding to the will of Alexander, who left his kingdom to the worthiest,[9] Satan refers to the sort of kings whose conventional attributes are imperiousness and pride. In the third and final section of his speech (3. 227–50) Satan introduces the offer of Parthia: "Perhaps

thou linger'st in deep thoughts detained/ Of the enterprise so hazard-
ous and high."

The genuineness of Satan's contrition is obviously the crucial question here: first of all, the structure of the passage has been used to
dispute his sincerity. Viewing the opening as a preparation for the
second section of the speech, Mrs. Lewalski contends that from the
beginning Satan is trying to avoid the "worst" by corrupting Jesus, that
Satan is "audac[ious]" in requesting salvation, and that, manipulating
his outburst in order to hasten Jesus, Satan displays "rhetorical
craft." [10] One reason for preferring an alternative reading is that the
emotional emphasis does not support Mrs. Lewalski's view of the
structure. If Satan were preparing for a rhetorical climax in the center
of his speech, the climax would be more emphatic than the preparatory
buildup; yet "I would be at the worst" is clearly more passionate than
"If I then to the worst that can be haste." The argumentative connections also tell against the reading. Were Satan adding application to
exposition, the two units would match; but Satan's indifference to
Jesus' reign does not tally with his renewed call for zeal and duty, and
his praise of the savior's qualities does not correlate with his tribute
to the emperor.

The discrepancies suggest that Satan's transition, "If I then to the
worst that can be haste," is not a bit of "rhetorical craft," as Mrs.
Lewalski suggests, but a makeshift return from an unpremeditated
outcry, an outcry which Satan has decided to repudiate. The alternative to Mrs. Lewalski's reading is the view adopted by Stein. He suggests that the first section of the speech constitutes a pause in Satan's
assault, and that the second section is a return to Satan's usual arguments: "The spell is broken and the tempter goes back to his job." [11]
Not only can this view account for the emotional weight of the opening
and the intellectual disjunction between the adjacent sections, but it
can explain why in the second section Satan returns to the arguments
of the offer of Israel.

The content of the speech has also been used to dismiss Satan's cry
of remorse. Allen contends that "Satan's contrition is patently false":
the stated hopelessness—he argues—is inconsistent with the temptation of Jesus, and Satan's claim that he has "no fear" is contradicted
by his admitted fear both of the Father and of the fires of hell.[12] If
Satan's words were a persuasive or a rational snare designed to move
or deceive Jesus into sin, then logical inconsistency would invalidate
the arguments. But if, as Stein says, Satan's "performance" is "gratui-
tous," [13] an expression of anguish, guilt, and longing, then inconsist-

encies are not a proof of lying. A man whose mind and will are committed to a course may pursue it even if he feels no hope, and he may pause in the pursuit to mourn its futility. Even if he fears execution, he may resign himself to it from the pain of waiting; and even knowing that his case is beyond appeal he may desire and imagine pardon.

Allen's argument is not compelling, then, and there is evidence which supports a contrary reading. Satan's hopelessness, it is true, is open to question. His expression of sorrow ("All hope is lost/ Of my reception into grace; what worse?") might be construed as a repetition of his meretricious plea from the first day (Jesus labels it a lie [1. 407–8]): "This wounds me most (what can it less?) that man,/ Man fall'n shall be restored, I never more" (1. 404–5). Surely, though, the coy parenthesis and stagy antithesis of the passional seducer contrast with Satan's directness here. Nor is the repetition which Satan uses later an example of insincere rhetoric, a smooth synonymia; it is the tautology of passion: "worst is my port,/ My harbor and my ultimate repose,/ The end I would attain, my final good."

But if this passage is ambiguous, Satan's expression of longing is demonstrably sincere. When Satan addresses Jesus as the Son, he accepts for the moment what he had doubted before (1. 89–93), and what he will later continue to doubt (4. 196–205). He cannot be lying. Satan understands that Jesus might be identical with the Father's "first-begot," but he knows the Son only as the wielder of "fierce thunder" (1. 89–90). He could pretend, therefore, to believe that Jesus was his ordained scourge, but he cannot pretend to accept what he has never understood, that Jesus is to "work redemption" by—as Jesus says—taking "upon [his] head" the "full weight" of man's sins (1. 263–67). Disbelief had hindered Satan (1. 80–83) when Jesus, through his faith in the prophet's words, identified the descending dove (1. 280–82); so faith in the Bible's prophecies has allowed Jesus to understand the nature of his mission, while lack of faith has blocked Satan's understanding.[14] When Satan thinks of Jesus as a shelter from God's wrath, he expresses a new insight, and that insight could only have come to him in a moment of faith. The previous admission of guilt, equally unique, is authenticated by this pious sequel.

There are, then, reasons to read Satan's outcry not as a set of lies whose contradictions expose them, but rather as the manifestation of what Stein calls "an extraordinary moment," [15] a moment of "genuine agony" on Satan's part [16] which culminates in insight: "drop[ping] his 'rational' obsession over the problem of Christ's kingdom," Satan "imagines, or intuits" Jesus' "sacrificial role"—the role "so far un-

imagined and about to disappear again from the scene of consciousness." [17]

Northrop Frye questions the truth of the insight.[18] Claiming that
Satan's image of the interposing cloud presents "the direct opposite
of Christ's true nature," Frye quotes from *Paradise Lost* the angels' song
of tribute to the Son, "In whose conspicuous count'nance without
cloud/ Made visible, Th' Almighty Father shines." [19] Satan's faulty
knowledge would at least cast doubt on the depth of his contrition—
it might even suggest his insincerity—but Frye's deprecation is ill-
founded. Satan's view of the Son as savior tallies with Jesus' own belief,
and the linking is reinforced by a momentary ironic contrast of Satan
with Jesus' followers: in his moment of faith the condemned Satan
exceeds the saved in knowledge. Satan's imagery is not an authorial
allusion to *Paradise Lost* but a character's recollection of the Bible: the
God who "will not at all acquit the wicked," says Nahum, "hath his
way in the whirlwind and in the storm," and "his fury is poured out
like fire," [20] but God is also, according to Isaiah, "a refuge from the
storm, a shadow from the heat." [21] The image both explains and veri-
fies Satan's vision. The desert surroundings remind desolate Satan of
a biblical warning, and in an instant of faith he remembers and understands his only means of escape. The prophets who informed Jesus
of his mission inform Satan in his moment of belief.

Thus in the second day's climactic shift of stance, the victim attacks
and the attacker suddenly—though temporarily—surrenders. It is
natural to see Satan's first reaction as suicidal despair—that is Stein's
reading [22]—but the differences between Satan's present feelings and
their analogues in the past suggest that Satan's state is less akin to
despair than to resignation in suffering. The last word of Jesus' speech,
"destruction," calls up the sense of defeat and the self-disgust which
Satan had experienced after his first encounter with Jesus; now, however, Satan is intense, agonized, rather than depressed. The pain
causes Satan to remember the ages of apprehension which he had
described during the first assembly; but here again Satan responds in
a new way, for earlier he had traveled reluctantly to the "harbor" he
now seeks:

> Long the decrees of Heav'n
> Delay, for longest time to him is short;
> And now too soon for us the circling hours
> This dreaded time have compassed.
>
> (1. 55–59)

After this renewal of Satan's sensory soul, his reason opens to the whole of Jesus' argument. In reply to Jesus' question, "What concerns it thee when I begin . . . ?" (3. 198–99), Satan answers that it concerns him not at all: "[My crime] will alike be punished, whether thou/ Reign or reign not." Replying to Jesus' declaration that Satan will fall, Satan admits the justice of the fall: "My error was my error, and my crime/ My crime." Satan surrenders his hold on the world for an instant, and interrupts his dispersion of crime and error. This moment of rational virtue is succeeded by the interval of faith during which Satan glimpses salvation. The ascent of virtue here is the reverse of that step-by-step deterioration which constitutes Satan's development.

When Jesus speaks as "Israel's true king," Satan hears and bows; his moment of rectitude proves the reality of Jesus' rule, the power of Jesus' instruction. The climax is forceful partly because of the interaction of dramatic with schematic patterning. Not only is Jesus' attack a surprising answer to an unemphatic offer, but Satan's reactions contrast with his qualities as a rational tempter: Satan's emotional exhaustion, and the sophistry and spiritual blindness of his offers serve as foils to his present agony, guilt, and longing. Partly, though, the climax is powerful for dramatic reasons alone, for its new revelations about the central characters: narrow Satan shows his potential breadth, and Jesus displays his royal authority.

Balanced against the vindication of Jesus' rule is Satan's continuing deterioration. Two passages indicate the progressive nature of the decline, showing the passional ruin which has resulted from Satan's sensory trial of Jesus. During the first temptation Satan could still muster self-control in the service of evil: though "inly stung with anger and disdain" he could still "Dissemble[ ]" (1. 465–67). Now there are important lapses in that control, the first of them the fit of temper which follows Jesus' elegant refusal of Satan's banquet. Satan, "malcontent" (2. 392), asserts his own power (2. 393–98) in answer to Jesus' tantalizingly paradoxical assertions of what befits the Son of God (2. 279–88). In replying to Jesus' charge that his "specious gifts" are "guiles" (2. 391), Satan speaks as injured innocence: "I see/ What I can do or say is suspect" (2. 399); and he defends as "far-fet spoil" (2. 400–401) the "pompous delicacies" which Jesus has disdained (2. 390).

This retort is not—as Mrs. Lewalski holds—a "casual counterclaim," [23] for Satan's words and deeds expose him. What Satan had called the creatures' gift to the Son (2. 324–27) he now labels the devil's tender, and he reveals that what he had termed the bounty of innocent nature (2. 331–36) is the devil's ware. Defending his banquet, he admits that the food is excessive ("far-fet") and sumptuous ("spoil"). His petulant disposal of the gifts justifies Jesus' prudent rejection of them. By comparing the devil's seizure to the "sound of harpies' wings and talons" (2. 403), Milton implies that Satan has exposed his enmity to Jesus (he alludes, of course, to the harpies which harassed Aeneas); [24] and the disappearance of the table (2. 401–2) symbolizes and reveals the transience of the sort of power which Satan has offered. Only temper can account for Satan's self-defeating activity; the new kind of lapse marks a change in passional state.

After Jesus' refusal of the offer of Rome, Satan names the price for his kingdoms (4. 155–69). Mrs. Lewalski claims that by this display of audacity Satan is trying to save face, that he is enhancing the value of his rejected kingdoms by attaching a high price to them. The maneuver would be—as Mrs. Lewalski says—a "desperate" one,[25] for a reason which Stein supplies: "A bargainer like Satan" would "not expect a customer uninterested in the merchandise to become interested on hearing the full price." [26] Yet Milton does not say that Satan replies "desperate," he says that he replies "impudent" (4. 154): the word suggests that Satan is taunting Jesus rather than tempting him. Stein claims that the taunts have an ulterior purpose: Satan hopes to provoke Jesus into declaring his identity.[27] But Stein has difficulty in explaining Satan's reaction to Jesus' indignant "Get thee behind me" (4. 193); he must argue that Satan "is 'with fear abasht,' but not too abashed, at the failure of his overt impiousness." [28]

In specifying that Satan replies "with fear abashed" (4. 195), Milton is not minimizing the fear; and the fact that Satan reacts to Jesus' reprimand ("Be not so sore offended") suggests that the cause of his reaction is not the failure of his tactic but the command of Jesus. The response proves that Satan has not provoked Jesus intentionally. Afterward, it is true, Satan claims to have been testing the identity of his adversary (4. 196–205), but the fact that he is improvising an excuse is suggested not only by his fear but by his search for a loophole: he appeals to Jesus' statement that God has permitted Satan the trier's role (4. 174–75). Satan's taunt is a second fit of temper, then—an expression of frustration at the failure of the last of his planned baits, an expression of anger that Jesus has perceived his plight.

Frustrated and angry, Satan says to Jesus what he would have said had Jesus accepted Rome. He produces an insulting display of self-aggrandizement, combining his first day's claim to be man's "Copartner" and "disposer" (1. 387–93) with Jesus' own contention that it is more "magnanimous" to "give a kingdom" than to "assume" one (2. 481–83):

> All these which in a moment thou behold'st
> The kingdoms of the world, to thee I give;
> For giv'n to me, I give to whom I please,
> No trifle.

Continuing with his "condition," that Jesus "fall down/ And worship [him] as [his] superior lord," Satan demands the sort of allegiance paid by provincial kings to the emperor at Rome: Jesus is to become Satan's vassal. The outburst exposes the intention behind the offers of worldly rule, and in order to retrieve the situation, Satan is forced to make a further disclosure, the admission that he wishes to learn Jesus' relation to the heavenly Son.

During the second temptation Satan adds rational exhaustion to the sensory ruin brought him by his first assault. The story of his rational decline is organized around two turning points; the first and major one is Satan's recovery from his moment of remorse. Before Jesus' counterattack Satan has revealed his rational limitations in his ranking of what he offers. The order of the specific kingdoms is not explainable on schematic grounds: there is no logical reason for the spiritual kingdom to precede the bestial one. The order must be accounted for in terms of character: it is a sign of Satan's obsessive worldliness. Despite the fact that he remembers Daniel's prophecy of the statue and the shattering stone,[29] Satan cannot believe in the importance of Israel: he offers it first because it seems insignificant to him—"small," as Stein says, "and both politically and strategically unimportant."[30]

After Jesus' counterattack, Satan reveals the same limitations, repeating for the offers of Parthia and Rome the argumentative motifs he had introduced in the offer of Israel. Now, however, the restriction is more serious: Satan has failed to see that his surrender to Israel's king has validated Jesus' rule and nullified any further offers. The moment of remorse presents Satan with an escape from restriction: he sees the foolishness of his plan to prevent Jesus' rule, and he distinguishes earthly rule from Jesus' role as savior. When he repudiates remorse and resumes his temptations ("If I then to the worst that can be haste") Satan dooms his reason. The episode resembles the poignant moment when, standing on Niphates' top, the Satan of *Paradise Lost* comes to the verge of contrition—"O then at last relent"— only to relapse: "So farewell hope, and with hope farewell fear,/ Farewell remorse!"[31]

The second turning point in Satan's rational decline follows Jesus' refusal of Rome. Having extenuated his loss of temper, Satan makes a new effort to understand his opponent (4. 209–21). He does not regain his former insight into Jesus' Sonship, neither does he experience his former guilt, but Satan does finally grasp what Jesus has told him about the nature of his rule. He sees that Jesus means to "rul[e] . . . by persuasion" (4. 229–35), and he rightly chooses a "democraty" as the state appropriate for him (4. 268–71). But as Satan lapsed earlier, so he hastens to misuse his understanding now, devising corruptions for this newly-comprehended kind of government.[32] Satan's first lapse is crucial, his second final.

Two passages measure the falls which succeed the two moments of understanding. The first passage is Satan's fit of temper after the rejection of Rome. This outburst is greater than its predecessor, for not only is the cause greater (the refusal of Rome is more significant than the refusal of the banquet), but the agent is weaker: in addition to his earlier passional corruption, Satan reveals the enfeeblement of his reason. The insulting offer to Jesus contrasts with the understanding Satan had attained in his moment of remorse. Boasting of the "high esteem" in which he holds his offered kingdoms (4. 160), Satan clings to the rule whose end he had accepted earlier, and instead of acknowledging his guilt and error, he voices evil proposals. Furthermore, though Satan does sneer at Jesus' temperance ("Nothing will please the difficult and nice" [4. 157]), he is silent about Jesus' religious role. As Jesus reminds him, "if thou wilt fall down,/ And worship me as thy superior lord" has religious echoes; but "superior lord" is a political term, and "worship" can denote the sort of obeisance demanded by a Tiberius. Jesus' retort brings back the subject of religion, and Satan fashions an excuse from the rebuke, but the earlier forgetfulness is significant: Satan has returned to what Stein calls his " 'rational' obsession over the problem of Christ's kingdom."

Jesus' reply emphasizes Satan's enfeeblement. Jesus answers the sneer at his fastidiousness with a "nice" disdain of Satan's talk (4. 171–75) — a disdain whose patience contrasts with Satan's jeering: "But I endure the time, till which expired/ Thou hast permission on me." He closes his speech (4. 182–92) with an extensive treatment of the political implications of Satan's taunting proposal. Exploding Satan's claim that he is a magnanimous bestower of realms, Jesus terms him an ingrateful recipient ("how fairly is the Giver now/ Repaid!"); on the first day Jesus condemned Satan for appropriating God's revelations (1. 444–53), and now he blames him for "usurp[ing]" God's world. In reply to Satan's "condition," Jesus rebukes Satan for supposing that God's oracle would put the ruler of this world in the place of God. The response recalls Christ's answer to the Pharisees, "Render to Caesar the things that are Caesar's, and to God the things that are God's." [33]

The first main section of Jesus' speech (4. 176–81) is devoted to the religious implications of Satan's words, the way in which his "attempt" is "blasphémous." Jesus indignantly reminds Satan that he has forgotten "The first of all commandments," and, rebuking him for "dar[ing]" to "propound" to the "Son of God" to "worship [him] accurst," Jesus calls attention to the religious status of the two of them, the status which Satan in his worldliness has forgotten. That Jesus refers here to Satan's omissions is suggested by the structure of the speech. He does not take up Satan's argument until the final section —"The kingdoms of the world to thee were giv'n?"—and therefore his earlier statement must not be an explicit rebuttal. Furthermore, having discussed the religious meanings of the words "fall down/ And worship me," Jesus takes up the words a second time, relating them to Satan's claimed ownership of the world. By this he indicates that his first discussion had not touched upon the overt significance of the phrases. Jesus is most outraged by Satan's religious oblivion. Instead of treating the explicit meaning of Satan's statement, then examining the further ramifications, he begins with what is logically a later question: he is too indignant to wait. The attention paid to the religious forgetfulness is a reminder that Satan had once glimpsed Jesus' role as savior, and when Jesus pronounces Satan "more accurst" than ever, he refers to Satan's longing for a shelter from the Father's wrath. The subsequent rebuke to "usurp[ing]" Satan, to Satan "void of fear or shame," measures Satan's fall from his earlier renunciation and guilt.

As this passage relates to Satan's cry of contrition—to the first turning point—so the epilogue to the second day relates to the second turning point. Returning Jesus to the wilderness, Satan accuses him of otherworldly fanaticism ("What dost thou in this world?") and admits that Jesus has refused every imaginable worldly lure (4. 368–74). Then, attempting to save face, he makes an astrological prediction, reproaching Jesus for rejecting his offers (4. 374–81) and warning him of the consequences of the rejections (4. 382–93). The passage is repetitive in structure—it consists of a positive statement and a negative restatement of the same three points. The points, furthermore, are old ones, reiterations of the second day's arguments.[34] The redundancy and absence of new arguments are signs that, having perverted his last and hard-won insight, Satan is rationally exhausted.

The third section of Jesus' trial builds to the final tower scene, to

Jesus' triumphant demonstration of heroic faith. Since this section is eventful and brief, the intellectual preparations for the climactic episode are made earlier. The first words of Jesus (1. 196–200) express his awareness of the disparity between his declared and his "present state." These words establish Jesus' susceptibility to Satan's spiritual temptations generally, and in particular to Satan's final and fatal proposal, that Jesus should prove his identity by falling in confidence of rescue: "Cast thyself down, safely if Son of God" (4. 554–59). In the retrospective portion of his soliloquy, Jesus demonstrates his possession in theory of the martyr's courage he will need on the tower: the fact that the savior must face "many a hard assay even to the death" leaves him "neither . . . disheartened or dismayed" (1. 259–69). In the final section of his soliloquy, Jesus, finding himself led into a wilderness, resigns himself to God's will (1. 290–93). The action proves that Jesus has more than theoretical virtue, though the occasion does not call for the last degree of faith. On the pinnacle, Jesus, humanly liable to failure, realizes his perfect thoughts in perfect deeds.

During the last stage of Satan's decline, a repetition of motifs from the second stage indicates the cumulativeness of his decay. The display of temper which follows Jesus' refusal of the banquet is matched by the wrathful storm, and the outburst which ends the heart of the second day's offers has its parallel in Satan's "rag[ing]" (4. 499) introduction to the last of the third day's trials. Satan's ominous interpretation of the storm, the second incident on the final day, reuses the already stale arguments of the astrological prediction which closes the second temptation.[35] These reminiscences establish the permanence of Satan's emotional and rational collapse. To these earlier losses Satan adds, in his fall from the tower, the loss of the intellectual power which is his last resource.

Satan's fall is threefold: he falls like Antaeus (4. 562–71), he falls like the Sphinx (4. 572–80), he falls while Jesus is carried aloft (4. 581–85). The triple fall correlates with Satan's threefold vitiation. The two extended similes describe Satan's passional and rational destruction. Both images have emblematic potentialities: Oedipus is a classical byword for intelligence, and, as Mrs. Lewalski points out, the defeat of Antaeus is a common image for the conquest of "sensual or earthbound passions and desires."[36]

The applications of the similes support these conventional associations. The fall of Antaeus is likened to the fall of Satan "smitten with amazement." The astonishment relates to Satan's expectations as a sensory tempter—the expectations he voices when he sarcastically tells Jesus that "to stand upright/ Will ask [him] skill" (4. 551–52). The fall of the Sphinx is likened to the fall of Satan "strook with dread and anguish" by the loss of his kingdoms. The basis of the comparison is partly of course that like the Sphinx Satan tricks and ruins men, but the image also contains a specific reference to Satan's final test of Jesus' reason: "I to thy [f]ather's house/ Have brought thee, and highest placed; highest is best,/ Now show thy progeny" (4. 552–54). Like the Sphinx, Satan plays the riddler: he makes a metaphor out of Jesus' placement on the tower, quibbles on "[f]ather's house" and "highest placed," and invites a self-contradictory answer.[37] But though the images treat Satan as an embodiment of corrupt passion and corrupt reason, Milton in his descriptions refers to Satan as the type of intellectual corruption: Satan is the "Tempter proud," he dares to "proudly tempt the Son of God."

The subordinate aspects of Satan's defeat are subsumed under the principal aspect, and Milton treats this aspect in his contrast of Satan and Jesus. Jesus' ascent fulfills Isaiah's promise that the faithful will escape the curse meted out to disobedient mankind;[38] the ascent thus symbolizes Jesus' intellectual victory, and Satan's fall represents the antithetical intellectual defeat, the breaking of Satan's perverted will. Although this aspect of the fall is the principal one, Milton does not emphasize it imagistically; he returns to the subject, however, in the subsequent angelic hymn: the angels follow their tribute to Jesus' intellectual triumph with an emphatic announcement of Satan's intellectual destruction (4. 618–32). Milton mutes his first treatment lest it undercut the second.

Satan's fall from the tower entails a double set of ironies. First of all, in tempting Jesus, Satan brings about the opposite of what he intends. Satan sarcastically tells Jesus to "stand upright," and Jesus does. He riddlingly proposes that Jesus stand "highest" at his "[f]ather's house," and Jesus is accordingly enthroned. Satan treacherously invokes a text which promises an angelic rescue for the faithful, and Jesus is carried off by angels. The second set of ironies lies in the fact that Satan brings upon himself the injuries he intends for Jesus. Hoping that Jesus will display intemperance in his fall from the tower, Satan himself plummets from the roof, overcome by uncontrollable "amazement." Expecting to deprive Jesus of the world, Satan loses the world. Expecting that, declaring his identity, Jesus will die shorn of divine favor, Satan, attesting Jesus' divinity, falls paralyzed to hell. The last two instances relate to Satan's initial announcement of his objectives, and draw to a close the subject of Satan's aims.

By the end of his first encounter with Jesus, Satan is already worried about his realm. Addressing his council on the first day, Satan had described Jesus' supposed ambitions, to appear "in the head of nations . . . Their king, their leader, and supreme on earth" (1. 94–99). Returning from the first temptation, he lists his opponent's "gifts," and places greatest weight on Jesus' ability as a conqueror: "Perfections absolute, graces divine,/ And amplitude of mind to greatest deeds" (2. 137–39). Satan now believes that Jesus is as able as he is ambitious. But Satan is not yet convinced that he cannot defraud Jesus of his kingdom. While refuting Belial, he mentions Alexander and Scipio (2. 196–200)—he is thinking of the tack he will take with Jesus, to whom he later cites these heroes (3. 31–36)—and he ends by predicting that worldly lures will succeed where passional allurements failed (2. 225–34). The end of the day brings the defeat of Satan's attempt, but there is still one humiliation which he has escaped. The fact that on the last day Satan omits his customary prior consultation suggests that he is unwilling to report to his followers that they are no longer "Regents and potentates, and kings, yea gods,/ Of many a pleasant realm and province wide" (1. 117–18). The rebounding of Satan's last assault on Jesus' rule forces Satan to return to his waiting council, and there he is compelled to publicly admit defeat.

In his opening council, Satan declares his resolve to discover Jesus' identity (1. 64–93):

> His first-begot we know, and sore have felt
> When his fierce thunder drove us to the deep;
> Who this is we must learn, for man he seems
> In all his lineaments, though in his face
> The glimpses of his Father's glory shine.

The initial confrontation does not give Satan proof of Jesus' identity, as Allen claims,[39] but it does jar Satan, for the reversals and qualifications in his report to the waiting devils betray his uncertainty:

> [I] find
> Far other labor to be undergone
> Than when I dealt with Adam first of men,
> Though Adam by his wife's allurement fell,
> However to this man inferior far,
> If he be man by mother's side at least.
>
> (2. 131–36)

Nevertheless, Satan is not convinced that a mortal can be the heavenly Son—he is not persuaded even by his own transitory moment of faith—and later that day he truthfully reveals to Jesus the intention of learning his identity. The pinnacle episode resolves the question. On this resolution the comment of Elizabeth Pope is apt: "Milton . . . had no intention of permitting the devil to go away unsatisfied and dubious, as he does in the *Ludus Coventriae*. As a writer, he would probably object to so lame and flat a resolution to the doubt motif: to bring the theme to a full and perfect conclusion within the poem, Satan obviously ought to be made aware of the Lord's true identity at the last, though not in any manner which he has foreseen, or which gratifies him in the least." [40] Failing to force Jesus to declare his divinity, Satan learns not that Jesus is concealing supernatural consciousness and powers, but that a mere man can defeat him as thoroughly as the heavenly Son once did. When the angels compare the victory of Jesus to his later victory at Gergesenes, where "all unarmed" he will drive the devils "with the terror of his voice," [41] the angels liken the human victory to the Son's expulsion of the apostate angels. Satan had expected to use Jesus' declaration of divinity to bring about his death and damnation. Instead, the knowledge of Jesus' Sonship brings Satan the foretaste of his own destruction and "death." The angels reveal that Satan's paralyzed fall to hell foretells his final unresisting ("Bound") exclusion from God, and they liken the defeat to a wound which, if not the "last and deadliest," is none the less a fatal wound.

The irony whereby Satan accomplishes the opposite of what he intends for Jesus accords with Milton's pronouncement that Satan "unweeting" fulfills God's purposes rather than his own (1. 126–28). The rationale for this sort of irony lies in the privative theory of evil, and the climactic example placed at the end of Satan's story suggests the moral of this story: that the values represented by Satan are contrary to the nature of the universe. The irony whereby the injuries which Satan intends for Jesus fall upon himself conveys the premise which underlies Satan's development; it epitomizes the process whereby Satan destroys his capacities by turning them to evil ends. The irony summarizes and explains the development which is here complete.

The first part of Jesus' story is his threefold trial. The second part, the angelic banquet, is his reward. The elements of the episode relate to Jesus' tests and hardships in the wilderness. The heavenly food which the angels present recalls Satan's request for miraculous bread; the fruits and drink call to mind the provisions of the banquet; and the green setting recalls by contrast the rigors of the storm—the reference to Jesus' "weari[ness]" reinforces the association, calling up that sleepless night (4. 586–93). When Jesus leaves the wilderness (4. 638–39), his return to men inverts Satan's pronouncement on Jesus' rejection of the world's kingdoms: "The wilderness/ For thee is fittest place" (4. 372–73). The tributes in the angelic hymn (4. 596–617) evoke Satan's requests that Jesus assert his Sonship and fulfill God's prophecies.

What Jesus receives contrasts in its purity with what Satan has offered or suggested. Jesus' refreshment is not self-indulgent, for, hungry and weary, he has need of what he takes; in eating he displays no improper attachment to the senses, for the fruits from the Garden represent the sensory fulfillments appropriate to man's nature. That Jesus returns "unobserved" and "private" suggests the disinterestedness of his rule, and he returns to his proper subjects, to people who need and want his instruction. Having refused to prove his Sonship, Jesus is identified by angels, and having refused to hurry God, Jesus finds that he has already brought to pass the prophesied salvation of mankind, that by defeating Satan he has "founded" man's "fairer Paradise."

Not only is what Jesus receives pure, it is also retributive: if not always (as Mrs. Lewalski says) "more exalted" than what he has refused,[42] it is at least compensatory. The "flowery bank" makes amends for the storm, "Ambrosial" fruits and drink are better than Satan's meats and wine, and a banquet outweighs a miraculous crust. Jesus returns to his "mother's house" because—as Satan has observed —he is the son of David "By mother's side" (3. 154): he receives his destined kingdom, the Israel of "willing hearts" (1. 222)—a kingdom more worthy than savage Parthia or worldly Rome. Finally, Jesus is rewarded for human faith; angels verify what he cannot remember of his previous existence, and he who wondered "How best the mighty work he might begin/ Of Saviour to mankind" (1. 185–88) finds that he has already begun his work. As Satan's defeat suggests the falsity of his values, Jesus' reward validates the temperance, justice, and holiness he represents.

Jesus' trials and Satan's concomitant degeneration are handled in a dramatically varied way. The treatments have dramatic justifications, most notably in the second temptation, where the intellectually repetitive arguments by which Satan recommends specific kingdoms take on an interest of character when viewed in the light of Satan's climactic moment of insight. But the variety in the dramatic patterning is also a means whereby dramatic materials are integrated with the schematic structure of the poem. Jesus' unshakable passional rectitude and Satan's passional ruin are both treated in episodes separated from the first temptation. This retrospective treatment prevents weight from falling on the exchanges which end the first day's trial, exchanges which are schematically subordinate to Satan's opening request for bread. If on one hand the schematic structure helps to emphasize the dramatic climax of the second day—Jesus' attack and Satan's response are both surprising in their context—the dramatic climax helps to emphasize the schematically central section of the second temptation, the middle offers which must outshine both the spectacle of Satan's banquet and the novelty of the offer of learning. In the third temptation, the straightforward dramatic buildup puts weight on the schematically most important final episode.

Although these instances are the central ones, the integration of dramatic and nondramatic elements extends to details. Milton characterizes the poem's antagonist by Satan's loss of self-control on the second day, but he locates the fits of temper in places which clarify the logical divisions of the second temptation. Milton makes symbolic use of Satan's unaccompanied appearance on the final day—Satan's "strength" is thereby specifically "Satanic"—but he does not neglect to suggest the motive for Satan's failure to consult his followers, nor does he forget to make dramatic use of the event. The orderly complexity of the poem substantiates Milton's own high estimate of his tour de force.

In the last of his imagistic passages—the pair of similes which describe Satan's fall from the tower—Milton compares his poem not as before to other epics, but to tragedies. The genre is evoked by the fall of a "proud" ruler as well as by the sort of incident whose name—*deus ex machina*—recalls the stage. But it is also evoked by the heroes named in the similes, Hercules and Oedipus; for Aristotle notes that the "finest tragedies" have concerned the stories of only a few houses.[43] Hercules is of course a Euripedean subject, and the house of Oedipus is one of Aristotle's examples.

As before, Milton implies the superiority of his own poem: to liken the fall of Antaeus to Satan's fall is "to compare/ Small things to greatest." The phrase is of course a tag, but again Milton invites a deeper comparison. First of all, he calls attention to the formal risks he has taken. Evoking tragedy at the moment that he resolves a dramatic situation with a *deus ex machina* intervention, Milton recalls Aristotle's strictures concerning mechanical resolutions.[44] Aristotle cites the arrival of Athena in the *Iliad* which prevents the lifting of the siege of Troy, and Milton averts his hero's death with a divine rescue. Aristotle cites the magical escape of Medea in Euripedes, and a band of angels releases Milton's hero from a trap. In addition, Milton brings up the old question of the ranking of the literary kinds. By juxtaposing epic and tragedy, he recalls that Aristotle, comparing the two genres, declared tragedy the greater.[45] The conjunction of genres is tightened by the opposed fates of the central characters. Aristotle associates this sort of double ending with the *Odyssey,* and declares it unsuitable for tragedies.[46] In suggesting that his epic is superior to tragedy, Milton claims that having taken great formal risks he has produced a poem more lofty than its kind, more lofty than the noblest of writings. In his sublime attempt, he has dared greatly, he says, and has succeeded.

Notes

Index

Notes

Chapter 1 Wedges

1. Arnold Stein, *Heroic Knowledge: An Interpretation of "Paradise Regained" and "Samson Agonistes"* (Minneapolis, 1957), pp. 6–7.

2. The prologue to the *Aeneid,* usually rejected now, usually accepted in the Renaissance: "Ille ego, qui quondam gracili modulatue avena/ Carmen."

3. The specific allusions are *Aeneid* 10. 690 ff., *Iliad* 16. 641 ff., *Odyssey* 1. 1 ff., *Le Morte Darthur* 6. 3, 4. 24, 14. 8–10.

4. *The Republic* 605. The passage relies on the division of the soul into the faculties of desire, will, and reason, while Milton's poem relies on a sense-reason-intellect division; but *mutatis mutandis* the passage applies, and it is evoked by Milton's repeated challenges.

5. Similar points are developed — from a different viewpoint and from different evidence — by Ralph W. Condee in "Milton's Dialogue with the Epic: *Paradise Regained* and the Tradition," *Yale Review* 59 (1969–70): 357–75.

6. E. M. W. Tillyard, *Milton* (London, 1930), pp. 316–18.

7. Louis L. Martz, *The Paradise Within: Studies in Vaughan, Traherne, and Milton* (New Haven, 1964), p. 175.

8. *Heroic Knowledge,* pp. 54–55.

9. Ibid., p. 78.

10. Elizabeth M. Pope, *"Paradise Regained": The Tradition and the Poem* (Baltimore, 1947), pp. 100–101.

11. Irene Samuel, *Plato and Milton* (Ithaca, 1947), pp. 70–71.

12. Barbara K. Lewalski, *Milton's Brief Epic: The Genre, Meaning, and Art of "Paradise Regained"* (Providence, 1966), pp. 219, 256, 281–82.

13. Northrop Frye, "The Typology of *Paradise Regained,*" *Modern Philology* 53 (1955–56): 230–34.

14. Howard Schultz, "Christ and Antichrist in *Paradise Regained,*" *PMLA* 67 (1952): 797n.

113

15. A. S. P. Woodhouse, "Theme and Pattern in *Paradise Regained*," *University of Toronto Quarterly* 25 (1955–56): 176.

16. *Milton's Brief Epic,* pp. 203–4, 215–16.

17. Dick Taylor, Jr., "The Storm Scene in *Paradise Regained:* A Reinterpretation," *University of Toronto Quarterly* 24 (1954–55): 360.

18. Allen H. Gilbert, "The Temptation in *Paradise Regained,*" *JEGP* 15 (1916): 603.

19. "The Storm Scene," pp. 365–71.

20. Ibid., p. 372.

21. See Pope, *"Paradise Regained": The Tradition and the Poem,* pp. 65–66, 67.

22. *Paradise Within,* p. 183.

23. Ibid., p. 199.

24. Ibid., pp. 199–200.

25. *Milton's Brief Epic,* pp. 113–14.

26. Ibid., p. 188.

27. Ibid., p. 195.

28. Ibid., p. 282.

29. Ibid., pp. 310–12.

30. Ibid., p. 310.

31. Ibid., p. 313.

32. Ibid., p. 310.

33. Ibid., pp. 306–7.

34. Ibid., pp. 317–18.

35. *"Paradise Regained": The Tradition and the Poem,* p. 29.

36. Irene Samuel, "Milton on Learning and Wisdom," *PMLA* 64 (1949): 718.

37. "The Temptation in *Paradise Regained,*" p. 606.

38. "Christ and Antichrist," p. 790.

39. *Milton's Brief Epic,* p. 275.

40. *Paradise Within,* pp. 190–91.

41. "Milton on Learning," p. 715*n.*

42. Schultz, "Christ and Antichrist," p. 803.

43. Ibid.

44. Ibid., pp. 799–800.

45. *"Paradise Regained": The Tradition and the Poem,* pp. 76–77.

46. *Milton's Brief Epic,* pp. 274–75.

47. B. Rajan, *"Paradise Lost" and the Seventeenth Century Reader* (London, 1947), p. 51.

48. See "Christ and Antichrist," p. 806.

49. See *Heroic Knowledge,* pp. 101–2.

50. *"Paradise Regained": The Tradition and the Poem,* p. 101.

51. "Christ and Antichrist," p. 797*n.*

52. Ibid.

53. *Heroic Knowledge,* p. 88. Stein refers specifically to 3. 223 ff.

54. "Christ and Antichrist," p. 798.

55. The tradition is treated in *"Paradise Regained": The Tradition and the Poem,* pp. 51–69; the quotation appears on p. 51.

56. *"Paradise Regained": The Tradition and the Poem,* pp. 98–101.

57. Ibid., pp. 51–54.

58. "Theme and Pattern," p. 175.

59. "The Temptation in *Paradise Regained,*" pp. 602–3.

60. *Milton's Brief Epic,* p. 202.

61. *"Paradise Regained": The Tradition and the Poem,* p. 99.

62. *Milton's Brief Epic,* p. 304.

63. *"Paradise Regained": The Tradition and the Poem,* p. 49–50.

64. Ibid., p. 76.

65. "Theme and Pattern," p. 175.

66. *Milton's Brief Epic,* pp. 224–27.

67. *Heroic Knowledge,* p. 23.

68. *Plato and Milton,* p. 159.

69. *The Republic* 581A.

70. *"Paradise Regained": The Tradition and the Poem,* pp. 67–69.

71. Baldesar Castiglione, *"The Book of the Courtier* 4. 51.

72. *Heroic Knowledge,* p. 46.

73. Ibid., p. 44.

74. Dick Taylor, Jr., "Grace as a Means of Poetry: Milton's Pattern for Salvation," *Tulane Studies in English* 4 (1954): 83.

75. *The Republic* 581A.

76. "Grace as a Means," p. 82.

77. Ibid., p. 83.

78. *"Paradise Regained": The Tradition and the Poem,* pp. 78–79.

79. *Heroic Knowledge,* pp. 9–10.

80. Ibid., p. 9.

Chapter 2 The First Try

1. Merritt Y. Hughes, "The Christ of *Paradise Regained* and the Renaissance Heroic Tradition," *Studies in Philology* 35 (1938): 258.

2. Northrop Frye, "The Typology of *Paradise Regained,"* *Modern Philology* 53 (1955–56): 229.

3. Arnold Stein, *Heroic Knowledge: An Interpretation of "Paradise Regained" and "Samson Agonistes"* (Minneapolis, 1957), p. 18.

4. *The Republic* 429, 441.

5. *Heroic Knowledge,* p. 27.

6. Ibid., p. 219, *n.* 17.

7. *Gorgias,* 507.

8. *Heroic Knowledge,* p. 24.

9. Ibid., p. 29.

10. A. S. P. Woodhouse, "Theme and Pattern in *Paradise Regained,"* *University of Toronto Quarterly* 25 (1955–56): 171–72.

11. *Heroic Knowledge,* p. 44.

12. Howard Schultz, "Christ and Antichrist in *Paradise Regained,"* *PMLA* 67 (1952): 796–97.

13. Elizabeth M. Pope, *"Paradise Regained": The Tradition and the Poem* (Baltimore, 1947), p. 47.

14. Ibid.

15. Ibid., p. 46.

16. The question mark which Bush places at the end of the second sentence is grammatically justified (the 1671 edition has a semicolon).

17. *Heroic Knowledge,* p. 44.

18. Dick Taylor, Jr., "Grace as a Means of Poetry: Milton's Pattern for Salvation," *Tulane Studies in English* 4 (1954): 87–88. The scene is treated in detail in chapter 5.

19. Deuteronomy 8:3.

20. Barbara K. Lewalski, *Milton's Brief Epic: The Genre, Meaning, and Art of "Paradise Regained"* (Providence, 1966), p. 212. The dispute over this passage is treated in chapter 6.

Chapter 3 The Evening and the Morning of the Second Day

1. Elizabeth M. Pope, *"Paradise Regained": The Tradition and the Poem* (Baltimore, 1947), p. 71.

2. Barbara K. Lewalski, *Milton's Brief Epic: The Genre, Meaning, and Art of "Paradise Regained"* (Providence, 1966), p. 217.

3. Ibid., pp. 221–22.

4. Northrop Frye, "The Typology of *Paradise Regained,*" *Modern Philology* 53 (1955–56): 232.

5. The contrary interpretation by Arnold Stein (*Heroic Knowledge: An Interpretation of "Paradise Regained" and "Samson Agonistes"* [Minneapolis, 1957], pp. 92–93) is disputed in chapter 7.

6. Lewalski, *Milton's Brief Epic,* p. 289.

7. Carey so annotates the line in *The Poems of John Milton,* ed. John Carey and Alastair Fowler (London and Harlow, 1968), p. 1149n.

8. Proverbs 8:1–10, 10:11, 13:14.

9. The line is usually taken as referring to the suspension of the construction of Philo's dockyard, but Carey notes (*Poems of John Milton,* p. 1148n) that in dispute of this interpretation of Baldwin's, Wright has glossed the word "shook" as "brandished, as the symbol of Athenian naval power." This gloss better fits the context.

10. "[M]any books . . . are wearisome" alludes to Ecclesiastes 12:12. "He who receives/ Light from above, from the Fountain of Light,/ No other doctrine needs" recalls James 1:17: "Every good gift and every perfect gift is from above, and cometh down from the Father of lights." Since this allusion would be anachronistic, the point must be that Jesus is alluding to the texts which underlie James's words. Psalms 119:130–31 comes closest to Jesus' lines: "The entrance of thy words giveth light; it giveth understanding unto the simple. I opened my mouth, and panted: for I longed for thy commandments." Jesus' "Fountain" means "source," in parallel to James's "Father," but "Fountain" also compares the rays of the sun to a stream. The text in Psalms similarly joins light and water.

11. *Milton's Brief Epic,* p. 224.

12. Ibid., p. 225.

13. Sir Thomas Malory, *Le Morte Darthur* 14. 8–10.

14. *Milton's Brief Epic,* pp. 224–25.

15. *Le Morte Darthur* 6. 3, 4. 24.

16. Ibid., 21. 6.

17. Proverbs 23:1–3. Satan in replying refers to Daniel 1:1–16.

18. Michael Fixler, "The Unclean Meats of the Mosaic Law and the Banquet Scene in *Paradise Regained,*" *Modern Language Notes* 70 (1955): 576.

19. *Milton's Brief Epic,* pp. 216–17.

20. "Unclean Meats," p. 576.

21. *Milton's Brief Epic,* pp. 221–22.

22. "Unclean Meats," p. 575.

23. *Milton's Brief Epic,* p. 216.

24. "Unclean Meats," p. 574.

25. *Milton's Brief Epic,* p. 216.

26. Psalms 78, 91.

27. *"Paradise Regained": The Tradition and the Poem,* p. 78.

28. Ibid., p. 79.

29. The passage from Book One is discussed in the preceding chapter.

30. Don Cameron Allen, *The Harmonious Vision* (Baltimore, 1954), p. 113.

31. *Heroic Knowledge,* p. 57.

Chapter 4 The Heart of the Offer of Kingdom

1. Barbara K. Lewalski argues that Satan wants Jesus to identify himself with an inferior type of kingly temperance, Hercules; Alexander, Scipio, Caesar, and Pompey, she says, are compared to Hercules in classical times, and Hercules is a type of Christ (*Milton's Brief Epic: The Genre, Meaning, and Art of "Paradise Regained"* [Providence, 1966], pp. 229–39). Mrs. Lewalski does not provide sufficient evidence that Milton draws upon the typology she describes: as she admits, Hercules is not mentioned at this point in the poem, and though, as she says, Hercules *is* sometimes associated with banquets (p. 230), Milton does not evoke him here, alluding instead to assorted demigods, nymphs, and Arthurian knights (2. 350–61). Furthermore, in order to treat the historical figures as typological symbols, Mrs. Lewalski must ignore the specific arguments voiced by Satan and Jesus, and the argumentative functions of the figures they name.

2. The passages from Book Two are discussed in chapter 3.

3. Haggai 2:8, cited by Carey in *The Poems of John Milton,* ed. John Carey and Alastair Fowler (London and Harlow, 1968), p. 1113*n.*

4. Utilizing a formula from the Roman Missal, Milton suggests that Satan is quoting the ritualistic Pharisees.

5. For example, Merritt Y. Hughes cites Carolus Martellus (*John Milton: Complete Poems and Major Prose* [New York, 1958], p. 505*n*), and Douglas Bush cites Diocletian, Emperor Charles V, and Queen Christina of Sweden (*The Complete Poetical Works of John Milton* [Boston, 1965], p. 486*n*).

6. Judges 8:22–23, 1 Samuel 8.

7. 1 Samuel 9:9.

8. Judges 7.

9. 1 Samuel 2:7–8.

10. 1 Samuel 2:30.

11. Daniel 2:31–38.

12. Carey comments that the word *"luxurious"* fits the city better than it fits the kings (*Poems of John Milton,* p. 1129*n*).

13. Arnold Stein, *Heroic Knowledge: An Interpretation of "Paradise Regained" and "Samson Agonistes"* (Minneapolis, 1957), p. 89.

14. Bush (*Complete Poetical Works,* p. 490*n*) and Carey (*Poems of John Milton,* p. 1123*n*) cite Psalm 69.

15. *Milton's Brief Epic,* p. 257.

16. A. S. P. Woodhouse, "Theme and Pattern in *Paradise Regained," University of Toronto Quarterly* 25 (1955–56): 173–74.

17. Daniel 2:21.

18. Jeremiah 17:5–8. The texts are quoted later in the chapter.

19. *Heroic Knowledge,* p. 90.

20. Daniel 2:31–45.

21. *Milton's Brief Epic*, p. 268.

22. *Heroic Knowledge*, p. 92. Stein was the first to point out that Jesus is frequently urbane, and I am indebted to him for the general point as well as for this detail.

23. Elizabeth M. Pope, *"Paradise Regained": The Tradition and the Poem* (Baltimore, 1947), p. 39.

24. Ibid., p. 22.

25. Ibid., p. 38.

26. *Milton's Brief Epic*, p. 260.

27. Matthew 24:36.

28. Mrs. Lewalski's contrary interpretation (*Milton's Brief Epic*, p. 260) is discussed in chapter 6.

29. Daniel 4:10–12.

30. Ecclesiastes 3:1.

Chapter 5 Ascension Day

1. Dick Taylor, Jr., "Grace as a Means of Poetry: Milton's Pattern for Salvation," *Tulane Studies in English* 4 (1954): 86.

2. Dick Taylor, Jr., "The Storm Scene in *Paradise Regained:* A Reinterpretation," *University of Toronto Quarterly* 24 (1954–55): 360; the theory is discussed in chapter 1.

3. "Grace as a Means," pp. 86–87.

4. Don Cameron Allen, *The Harmonious Vision* (Baltimore, 1954), pp. 114–15.

5. Arnold Stein, *Heroic Knowledge: An Interpretation of "Paradise Regained" and "Samson Agonistes"* (Minneapolis, 1957), p. 116.

6. Ibid., p. 126.

7. Proverbs 28:18.

8. Psalms 91:11–12.

9. Proverbs 4:5, 4:26, 4:27.

10. Jesus walks "Backed on the north and west by a thick wood" (4. 448). North is the devil's domain (Isaiah 14:13), west is associated with death, and a grove on a hill is a place for idolatry (Jeremiah 17:2): Jesus removes his foot from evil. While Satan "talk[s]" Jesus "[goes] on/ And stay[s] not" (4. 484–85): he turns not to the right hand nor to the left.

11. *Heroic Knowledge*, p. 119.

12. Logically the sentence should end with a rhetorical question: "'Thou wouldst not gain thy kingdom?" Satan substitutes a declaration for the question, and a sarcastic positive statement for the negative one.

13. Elizabeth M. Pope, *"Paradise Regained": The Tradition and the Poem* (Baltimore, 1947), pp. 80–83.

14. Ibid., p. 85.

15. John Carey and Alastair Fowler, eds., *The Poems of John Milton* (London and Harlow, 1968), p. 1162n.

16. *Harmonious Vision*, p. 115.

17. *"Paradise Regained": The Tradition and the Poem*, p. 103.

18. Here and elsewhere I alter Bush's capitalization in this important line in accord with my rather unconventional reading.

19. Barbara K. Lewalski, *Milton's Brief Epic: The Genre, Meaning, and Art of "Paradise Regained"* (Providence, 1966), pp. 315–16.

20. *"Paradise Regained": The Tradition and the Poem*, pp. 93–94.

21. This point is argued at length in chapter 6.

22. *"Paradise Regained": The Tradition and the Poem,* p. 103.

23. "Grace as a Means," p. 87; *Heroic Knowledge,* p. 127.

24. "Grace as a Means," pp. 86–87.

25. *Heroic Knowledge,* p. 127.

26. Allen H. Gilbert, "The Temptation in *Paradise Regained,"JEGP* 15 (1916): 609–10.

27. Acts 7:47.

28. The first day's event is discussed in chapter 2.

29. A. S. P. Woodhouse, "Theme and Pattern in *Paradise Regained,"* *University of Toronto Quarterly* 25 (1955–56): 181.

30. *"Paradise Regained": The Tradition and the Poem,* p. 103; see also Miss Pope's comments on the sensationalism of the scene, pp. 96–97.

31. "Theme and Pattern," p. 181.

32. *"Paradise Regained": The Tradition and the Poem,* pp. 103–4.

33. "Theme and Pattern," p. 181.

34. *Samson Agonistes,* 1371–1426.

35. "Grace as a Means," p. 88*n.*

36. *Milton's Brief Epic,* p. 316.

37. Ibid.

38. Ibid., pp. 315–16.

39. Ibid.

40. *Heroic Knowledge,* pp. 128–29.

41. Ibid., p. 128.

42. Traditionally — John M. Steadman argues — the fruits from the Tree of Life are a type of eternal life, a reward for obedience, and a symbol of the Messiah's redemptive role (*Milton's Epic Characters: Image and Idol* [Chapel Hill, 1968], pp. 84–89). But by relating the fruits to Jesus' hunger and weariness — to his physical needs — Milton restricts the symbolic suggestiveness; he makes the fruits mere food, though Edenic food.

43. "Grace as a Means," p. 88.

44. Psalms 91:14. This is part of the psalm which Satan quotes, and it is related to the text from Samuel to which Jesus refers during his pronouncement on glory.

45. Psalms 37:11.

46. Psalms 56:11–13. This and the preceding two texts from Psalms lie behind the Beatitudes, which are the model for the paradoxical elaborations of biblical texts which Milton attributes to Jesus during the offer of kingdoms.

47. "Grace as a Means," p. 87.

48. Ibid., pp. 87–88.

49. *"Paradise Regained": The Tradition and the Poem,* pp. 81–82.

50. Ibid., p. 103.

Chapter 6 Wings

1. Arnold Stein, *Heroic Knowledge: An Interpretation of "Paradise Regained" and "Samson Agonistes"* (Minneapolis, 1957), p. 48.

2. Barbara K. Lewalski, *Milton's Brief Epic: The Genre, Meaning, and Art of "Paradise Regained"* (Providence, 1966), p. 133.

3. Don Cameron Allen, *The Harmonious Vision* (Baltimore, 1954), p. 117.

4. *Milton's Brief Epic,* p. 133.

5. These issues are discussed in chapter 1.

6. *Heroic Knowledge*, p. 133.

7. Ibid., pp. 38–41.

8. Northrop Frye, "The Typology of *Paradise Regained*," *Modern Philology* 53 (1955–56): 229.

9. *Heroic Knowledge*, p. 133.

10. Ibid., p. 132.

11. Ibid., p. 38.

12. Merritt Y. Hughes, "The Christ of *Paradise Regained* and the Renaissance Heroic Tradition," *Studies in Philology* 35 (1938): 257.

13. Claiming that Jesus denies all secular values and affirms only otherworldly ones, John M. Steadman argues that the poem relies on a traditional philosophic method, that of systematic rejection, and on a moral tradition, the tradition of moral choice imaged in the judgments of Paris and Hercules (*Milton's Epic Characters: Image and Idol* [Chapel Hill, 1968], pp. 123–36). But though Milton may well have known these traditions, he was free to ignore them, and the proof that he utilizes them is not very strong. For example, Steadman argues that, like Paris, Milton's Jesus examines the contemplative, active, and voluptuous lives (pp. 131–32), and that like Hercules he enters the wilderness and there chooses between alternative ways of life (pp. 125–26). These abstract likenesses cannot call up Paris or Hercules in a context so unredolent of naked goddesses and allegorical damsels; and Milton does not compare Jesus to Paris or refer to the story of Hercules' choice.

14. *Heroic Knowledge*, p. 17.

15. Howard Schultz, "Christ and Antichrist in *Paradise Regained*," *PMLA* 67 (1952): 790.

16. This passage is discussed in chapter 4.

17. Schultz applies the phrase to the sort of values he supposes to be embodied in the poem when it is read literally ("Christ and Antichrist," p. 791).

18. James H. Hanford, "The Temptation Motive in Milton," *Studies in Philology* 15 (1918): 181.

19. Elizabeth M. Pope, *"Paradise Regained": The Tradition and the Poem* (Baltimore, 1947), pp. 14–20.

20. Jackson I. Cope, *"Paradise Regained:* Inner Ritual," in *Milton Studies I*, ed. James D. Simmonds (Pittsburgh, 1969), p. 52. It is ingenious of Cope to praise as ritual what others deplore as lack of drama; nevertheless his case for ritualism is unconvincing. Contrasting ritual with drama, which is spatial and temporal, Cope argues that in *Paradise Regained* both space and time are negated. Space is negated by the metaphoric conversion of external conditions into internal states (e.g., "Thought following thought, and step by step led on" [1. 192]) and by the insubstantiality of Satan's "alleged temptations." These, says Cope, "do not appear as rounded, sensible substances, but as visions, illusions, histories, hints." Time is negated through Jesus' state of mind, for Jesus represents the atemporal faculty of the soul, the will, which "knows its end in its beginning." It follows, then, that in Jesus' "self-questionings" there is "no temptation, no drama, . . . only the formal recognition that man's and Satan's reason tempts and will corrupts — man." Jesus' will, Cope contends, is contrasted with Satan's reason. That faculty, temporal, "carries on dialogue, dialectic — it seeks to know" (ibid., pp. 61–64). As to the claim that Milton reduces space to thought, it should be noted that at times Milton moves outward from thought to space. "I as thou seest have none," says Jesus (2. 318), expressing his lack of need for food in terms which call attention to the barren

landscape (the line is discussed in chapter 3); "a kind of shading cool/ Interposition, as a summer's cloud," says Satan (3. 221–22), imaging the Son's intercession in terms which evoke the desert sky (the line is treated in chapter 7). If the one technique annihilates space, the other must re-create it. Cope's argument that Milton stresses the insubstantiality of Satan's offerings must be weighed against a contrary possibility. When E. M. W. Tillyard says that *"Paradise Regained* gets its effects largely by its pageantry" (*Milton* [London, 1930], p. 301), he suggests that through the banquet and the scenes Milton introduces visual elements into a setting which otherwise would provide no opportunities for description, and into a debate which otherwise would contain only abstractions. If there is any doubt as to which of these two effects Milton sought, consider the choices open to him. Elizabeth Pope lists eight theological explanations for how Satan showed the kingdoms of the world — among them that Satan presented the realms on a map, that he infiltrated Christ's imagination to create visions, that he pointed in the direction of the kingdoms and described them, and that he raised mirages (*"Paradise Regained": The Tradition and the Poem*, pp. 112–13). Any of these possibilities would have provided offerings less "rounded" and "sensible" than the ones Milton presents.

Cope argues the abolition of time by attributing to Jesus a constant mystical elevation which is at variance with Milton's portrayal — with, for example, Jesus' hunger, his early uncertainties about rule, the gaps in his knowledge of God's intentions. Cope deals with one of these examples: he calls Jesus' "self-questionings" ritualistic, "formal." But "Where will this end?" (2. 245) does not sound like the question of a man undertaking a ritual fast, and "Victorious deeds/ Flamed in my heart, heroic acts" (1. 215–16) is not a conventionalized recantation like "When I was a child . . . I thought as a child"; neither does "O what a multitude of thoughts at once/ Awakened in me swarm" sound undramatic, "formal." If such passages are Milton's way of representing a Jesus whose certitude is contrasted with mortal uncertainties, by what means could he have rendered a Jesus subject to human limitations and temptations?

21. George W. Whiting, "Christ's Miraculous Fast," *Modern Language Notes* 66 (1951): 15.

22. Ibid., pp. 12–13.

23. Ibid., pp. 13–15.

24. *"Paradise Regained": The Tradition and the Poem*, p. 22.

25. Ibid., pp. 34–38.

26. Ibid., p. 38.

27. Ibid., p. 39.

28. This passage is discussed in chapter 4.

29. *"Paradise Regained": The Tradition and the Poem*, p. 38.

30. Ibid.

31. This passage is discussed in chapter 4.

32. *"Paradise Regained": The Tradition and the Poem*, p. 39.

33. *Harmonious Vision*, p. 118.

34. *Milton's Brief Epic*, pp. 161–62.

35. *Harmonious Vision*, p. 119.

36. *Milton's Brief Epic*, p. 212.

37. Ibid., p. 213.

38. Micah 5. 12, cited by Carey, *The Poems of John Milton*, ed. John Carey and Alastair Fowler (London and Harlow, 1968), p. 1095*n*.

39. *Harmonious Vision*, p. 120; *Milton's Brief Epic*, p. 221.

40. *"Paradise Regained": The Tradition and the Poem,* p. 78.
41. *Milton's Brief Epic,* p. 221.
42. The speech is discussed in chapter 3.
43. *Milton's Brief Epic,* p. 260.
44. Daniel 4:10–12; Jesus' speech is discussed in chapter 4.
45. *Milton's Brief Epic,* pp. 160–61.
46. *Harmonious Vision,* p. 119; *Milton's Brief Epic,* pp. 214–15.
47. *Harmonious Vision,* p. 119.
48. *Milton's Brief Epic,* pp. 162–63.
49. Ibid., p. 213.
50. Ibid., p. 221.
51. Ibid., p. 135.
52. Ibid., p. 137.
53. Ibid., p. 161.
54. *Harmonious Vision,* pp. 119–20.
55. *Milton's Brief Epic,* p. 213.
56. Ibid., p. 214.
57. Ibid., p. 221.
58. *"Paradise Regained": The Tradition and the Poem,* p. 63.
59. I believe that God's offices and attributes provide the organizational basis of *Paradise Lost.* The creatures are judged by their relation to God's attributes, obedience and love being the most frequently mentioned virtues (with the first should be paired the recognition of God's superiority, and with the second the awe due to his wrath). Obedience is sometimes treated as the virtue appropriate to the reason, and love as the virtue appropriate to the passions. These equations, however, do not seem to me to be central to the poem's organization, and at any rate they would imply a two-part division of the soul, a division into the faculties of mind and heart, rather than the three-part division which underlies *Paradise Regained.* By his oppositions of reason and passion, faith and reason, however, one critic — Stanley Fish, to be exact — has suggested that a tripartite division of the soul is utilized in *Paradise Lost.* I disagree with him, but the issues raised by his case are too complicated for discussion here.
60. E. M. W. Tillyard, *Milton* (London, 1930), p. 305.
61. *"Paradise Regained": The Tradition and the Poem,* pp. 51–52.
62. *Harmonious Vision,* p. 111.
63. The matter of Satan's disguise is discussed in chapter 1.
64. The last three lines have a sharper point if viewed in terms of Eve's decision to garden separately in *Paradise Lost* particularly in terms of her last speech in the morning quarrel (9. 378–84): Eve was "rash" in her willing departure, "self-deceived" in believing that she could repulse the Tempter by herself. There are other lines in *Paradise Regained* whose points are sharpened by reference to *Paradise Lost,* but, given the disparity of the works in all important respects, it is doubtful that these minor references are a device for integrating the two poems. It is more likely that when Milton ran across an incidental theological point which he had considered earlier, he sometimes found it convenient to borrow the earlier solution. In this particular case, his comparison required an Eve who encountered the serpent not by accident but through a faulty decision of her own. Genesis does not tell how Eve came to be alone, and, as one critic has pointed out, the question has theological ramifications which Milton had to consider carefully. The solution of *Paradise Lost* was the detail required for the comparison in *Paradise Regained,* and therefore Milton referred to the earlier work. In this same random

way Milton makes oblique use in *Paradise Lost* of a few tenets from *De Doctrina* — mortalism, for instance, crops up in Adam's lament — but *Paradise Lost* is not a "sequel and companionpiece" to *De Doctrina.*

65. Isaiah 57:2.

66. *Heroic Knowledge*, p. 23; "Typology of *Paradise Regained,*" p. 237.

67. *Heroic Knowledge*, pp. 128–29; "Typology of *Paradise Regained,*" p. 237; the question is treated in chapter 5.

68. *Milton's Brief Epic*, p. 158.

69. *"Paradise Regained": The Tradition and the Poem*, pp. 31–34.

70. *Milton's Brief Epic*, p. 159.

71. *Harmonious Vision*, p. 111.

72. Ibid.

73. Ibid., p. 112.

74. This point is discussed at length in chapter 7.

75. *Harmonious Vision*, p. 111.

76. *Heroic Knowledge*, p. 11.

77. Isaiah 11:2.

78. *Harmonious Vision*, p. 120.

79. Ibid., p. 115.

Chapter 7 The Power of Darkness, the Power of the Son

1. *Gorgias* 507. This discussion relies on points raised in chapter 2.

2. The soliloquy is treated in the preceding chapter.

3. Don Cameron Allen, *The Harmonious Vision* (Baltimore, 1954), pp. 119–20.

4. Arnold Stein, *Heroic Knowledge: An Interpretation of "Paradise Regained" and "Samson Agonistes"* (Minneapolis, 1957), p. 54.

5. Ibid., pp. 49–50.

6. Ibid., p. 53.

7. Proverbs 23:1–3; the passage in Book Two is discussed in chapter 3.

8. Barbara K. Lewalski, *Milton's Brief Epic: The Genre, Meaning, and Art of "Paradise Regained"* (Providence, 1966), p. 257.

9. Pafford cites Quintus Curtius and Arrian as sources for this tale (William Shakespeare, *The Winter's Tale*, ed. J. H. P. Pafford [London, 1963], p. 137n).

10. *Milton's Brief Epic*, p. 258.

11. *Heroic Knowledge*, p. 87.

12. *Harmonious Vision*, p. 113.

13. *Heroic Knowledge*, p. 87.

14. The passages are discussed in chapter 6.

15. *Heroic Knowledge*, p. 84.

16. Ibid., p. 87.

17. Ibid., pp. 87–88.

18. Northrop Frye, "The Typology of *Paradise Regained,*" *Modern Philology* 53 (1955–56): 237.

19. *Paradise Lost* 3. 385–86.

20. Nahum 1:3, 1:6.

21. Isaiah 25:4.

22. Stein, *Heroic Knowledge*, pp. 85–86.

23. *Milton's Brief Epic*, p. 222.

24. *Aeneid* 3. 225 ff. Many editors also cite *Tempest* 3. 3. 52 S.D., but Ariel is a just avenger, a Fury, not a persecuting demon.

25. *Milton's Brief Epic*, p. 260.

26. *Heroic Knowledge*, p. 92.

27. Ibid., pp. 92–93.

28. Ibid., p. 94.

29. This matter is discussed in chapter 4.

30. *Heroic Knowledge*, p. 90.

31. *Paradise Lost* 4. 32–113. I am suggesting only a similarity in dramatic situation, not any continuity in character, or likeness in theological significance.

32. The speech is discussed in chapter 3.

33. Mark 12:17.

34. This point is treated in chapter 5.

35. This point is treated in chapter 5.

36. *Milton's Brief Epic*, p. 319.

37. This argument, like the previous references to the temptation speech, relies on arguments advanced in chapter 5.

38. "As on a floating couch" alludes to Isaiah 57:2; the point is discussed in chapter 6.

39. *Harmonious Vision*, p. 111; the issue is discussed in chapter 6.

40. Elizabeth M. Pope, *"Paradise Regained": The Tradition and the Poem* (Baltimore, 1947), p. 40.

41. Matthew 8:28–33.

42. *Milton's Brief Epic*, p. 114.

43. *Poetics* 1453A.

44. Ibid., 1454B.

45. Ibid., 1461B–62B.

46. Ibid., 1453A.

Index